Safety Symbols

These symbols appear in laboratory activities. They warn of possible dangers in the laboratory and remind you to work carefully.

 Safety Goggles Wear safety goggles to protect your eyes in any activity involving chemicals, flames or heating, or glassware.

 Lab Apron Wear a laboratory apron to protect your skin and clothing from damage.

 Breakage Handle breakable materials, such as glassware, with care. Do not touch broken glassware.

 Heat-Resistant Gloves Use an oven mitt or other hand protection when handling hot materials such as hot plates or hot glassware.

 Plastic Gloves Wear disposable plastic gloves when working with harmful chemicals and organisms. Keep your hands away from your face, and dispose of the gloves according to your teacher's instructions.

 Heating Use a clamp or tongs to pick up hot glassware. Do not touch hot objects with your bare hands.

 Flames Before you work with flames, tie back loose hair and clothing. Follow instructions from your teacher about lighting and extinguishing flames.

 No Flames When using flammable materials, make sure there are no flames, sparks, or other exposed heat sources present.

 Corrosive Chemical Avoid getting acid or other corrosive chemicals on your skin or clothing or in your eyes. Do not inhale the vapors. Wash your hands after the activity.

 Poison Do not let any poisonous chemical come into contact with your skin, and do not inhale its vapors. Wash your hands when you are finished with the activity.

 Fumes Work in a ventilated area when harmful vapors may be involved. Avoid inhaling vapors directly. Only test an odor when directed to do so by your teacher, and use a wafting motion to direct the vapor toward your nose.

 Sharp Object Scissors, scalpels, knives, needles, pins, and tacks can cut your skin. Always direct a sharp edge or point away from yourself and others.

 Animal Safety Treat live or preserved animals or animal parts with care to avoid harming the animals or yourself. Wash your hands when you are finished with the activity.

 Plant Safety Handle plants only as directed by your teacher. If you are allergic to certain plants, tell your teacher; do not do an activity involving those plants. Avoid touching harmful plants such as poison ivy. Wash your hands when you are finished with the activity.

 Electric Shock To avoid electric shock, never use electrical equipment around water, or when the equipment is wet or your hands are wet. Be sure cords are untangled and cannot trip anyone. Unplug equipment not in use.

 Physical Safety When an experiment involves physical activity, avoid injuring yourself or others. Alert your teacher if there is any reason you should not participate.

 Disposal Dispose of chemicals and other laboratory materials safely. Follow the instructions from your teacher.

 Hand Washing Wash your hands thoroughly when finished with an activity. Use antibacterial soap and warm water.

 General Safety Awareness When this symbol appears, follow the instructions provided. When you are asked to develop your own procedure in a lab, have your teacher approve your plan before you go further.

The Nature of Science and Technology

PRENTICE HALL Science Explorer

PEARSON

Prentice Hall

Needham, Massachusetts
Upper Saddle River, New Jersey

The Nature of Science and Technology

Book-Specific Resources

Student Edition
Interactive Textbook
Teacher's Edition
All-in-One Teaching Resources
Color Transparencies
Guided Reading and Study Workbook
Student Edition on Audio CD
Discovery Channel Video
Lab Activity Video
Consumable and Nonconsumable Materials Kits

Program Print Resources

Integrated Science Laboratory Manual
Computer Microscope Lab Manual
Inquiry Skills Activity Books
Progress Monitoring Assessments
Test Preparation Workbook
Test-Taking Tips With Transparencies
Teacher's ELL Handbook
Reading in the Content Area

Program Technology Resources

TeacherExpress™ CD-ROM
Interactive Textbook
Presentation Pro CD-ROM
ExamView®, Computer Test Bank CD-ROM
Lab zone™ Easy Planner CD-ROM
Probeware Lab Manual With CD-ROM
Computer Microscope and Lab Manual
Materials Ordering CD-ROM
Discovery Channel DVD Library
Lab Activity DVD Library
Web Site at PHSchool.com

Spanish Print Resources

Spanish Student Edition
Spanish Guided Reading and Study Workbook
Spanish Teaching Guide With Tests

Acknowledgments appear on p. 162, which constitutes an extension of this copyright page.

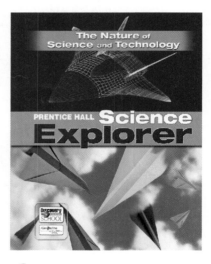

Cover
This model of a proposed spacecraft was generated on a computer (top). Colorful paper airplanes of different designs fly through the air (bottom).

ISBN 0-13-115380-3
2 3 4 5 6 7 8 9 10   08 07 06 05 04

Program Authors

Michael J. Padilla, Ph.D.
Professor of Science Education
University of Georgia
Athens, Georgia

Michael Padilla is a leader in middle school science education. He has served as an author and elected officer for the National Science Teachers Association and as a writer of the National Science Education Standards. As lead author of Science Explorer, Mike has inspired the team in developing a program that meets the needs of middle grades students, promotes science inquiry, and is aligned with the National Science Education Standards.

Ioannis Miaoulis, Ph.D.
President
Museum of Science
Boston, Massachusetts

Originally trained as a mechanical engineer, Ioannis Miaoulis is in the forefront of the national movement to increase technological literacy. As dean of the Tufts University School of Engineering, Dr. Miaoulis spearheaded the introduction of engineering into the Massachusetts curriculum. Currently he is working with school systems across the country to engage students in engineering activities and to foster discussions on the impact of science and technology on society.

Martha Cyr, Ph.D.
Director of K–12 Outreach
Worcester Polytechnic Institute
Worcester, Massachusetts

Martha Cyr is a noted expert in engineering outreach. She has over nine years of experience with programs and activities that emphasize the use of engineering principles, through hands-on projects, to excite and motivate students and teachers of mathematics and science in grades K–12. Her goal is to stimulate a continued interest in science and mathematics through engineering.

Book Authors

Andrew C. Kemp, Ph.D.
Assistant Professor of Education
University of Louisville
Louisville, Kentucky

Beth Miaoulis
Technology Writer
Sherborn, Massachusetts

Contributing Writer

Kenneth Welty, Ph.D.
Professor, School of Education
University of Wisconsin–Stout
Menomonie, Wisconsin

Consultants

Reading Consultant

Nancy Romance, Ph.D.
Professor of Science
    Education
Florida Atlantic University
Fort Lauderdale, Florida

Mathematics Consultant

William Tate, Ph.D.
Professor of Education and
    Applied Statistics and
    Computation
Washington University
St. Louis, Missouri

Reviewers

Teacher Reviewers

David R. Blakely
Arlington High School
Arlington, Massachusetts

Jane E. Callery
Two Rivers Magnet Middle
School
East Hartford, Connecticut

Melissa Lynn Cook
Oakland Mills High School
Columbia, Maryland

James Fattic
Southside Middle School
Anderson, Indiana

Dan Gabel
Hoover Middle School
Rockville, Maryland

Wayne Goates
Eisenhower Middle School
Goddard, Kansas

Katherine Bobay Graser
Mint Hill Middle School
Charlotte, North Carolina

Darcy Hampton
Deal Junior High School
Washington, D.C.

Karen Kelly
Pierce Middle School
Waterford, Michigan

David Kelso
Manchester High School Central
Manchester, New Hampshire

Benigno Lopez, Jr.
Sleepy Hill Middle School
Lakeland, Florida

Angie L. Matamoros, Ph.D.
ALM Consulting, INC.
Weston, Florida

Tim McCollum
Charleston Middle School
Charleston, Illinois

Bruce A. Mellin
Brooks School
North Andover, Massachusetts

Ella Jay Parfitt
Southeast Middle School
Baltimore, Maryland

Evelyn A. Pizzarello
Louis M. Klein Middle School
Harrison, New York

Kathleen M. Poe
Fletcher Middle School
Jacksonville, Florida

Shirley Rose
Lewis and Clark Middle School
Tulsa, Oklahoma

Linda Sandersen
Greenfield Middle School
Greenfield, Wisconsin

Mary E. Solan
Southwest Middle School
Charlotte, North Carolina

Mary Stewart
University of Tulsa
Tulsa, Oklahoma

Paul Swenson
Billings West High School
Billings, Montana

Thomas Vaughn
Arlington High School
Arlington, Massachusetts

Susan C. Zibell
Central Elementary
Simsbury, Connecticut

Safety Reviewers

W. H. Breazeale, Ph.D.
Department of Chemistry
College of Charleston
Charleston, South Carolina

Ruth Hathaway, Ph.D.
Hathaway Consulting
Cape Girardeau, Missouri

Douglas Mandt, M.S.
Science Education Consultant
Edgewood, Washington

Activity Field Testers

Nicki Bibbo
Witchcraft Heights School
Salem, Massachusetts

Rose-Marie Botting
Broward County Schools
Fort Lauderdale, Florida

Colleen Campos
Laredo Middle School
Aurora, Colorado

Elizabeth Chait
W. L. Chenery Middle School
Belmont, Massachusetts

Holly Estes
Hale Middle School
Stow, Massachusetts

Laura Hapgood
Plymouth Community
   Intermediate School
Plymouth, Massachusetts

Mary F. Lavin
Plymouth Community
   Intermediate School
Plymouth, Massachusetts

James MacNeil, Ph.D.
Cambridge, Massachusetts

Lauren Magruder
St. Michael's Country
   Day School
Newport, Rhode Island

Jeanne Maurand
Austin Preparatory School
Reading, Massachusetts

Joanne Jackson-Pelletier
Winman Junior High School
Warwick, Rhode Island

Warren Phillips
Plymouth Public Schools
Plymouth, Massachusetts

Carol Pirtle
Hale Middle School
Stow, Massachusetts

Kathleen M. Poe
Fletcher Middle School
Jacksonville, Florida

Cynthia B. Pope
Norfolk Public Schools
Norfolk, Virginia

Anne Scammell
Geneva Middle School
Geneva, New York

Karen Riley Sievers
Callanan Middle School
Des Moines, Iowa

David M. Smith
Eyer Middle School
Allentown, Pennsylvania

Gene Vitale
Parkland School
McHenry, Illinois

Contents

The Nature of Science and Technology

Reference Section

Enhance understanding through dynamic video.

Preview Get motivated with this introduction to the chapter content.

Field Trip Explore a real-world story related to the chapter content.

Assessment Review content and take an assessment.

Get connected to exciting Web resources in every lesson.

SciLINKS NSTA Find Web links on topics relating to every section.

Active Art Interact with selected visuals from every chapter online.

Planet Diary® Explore news and natural phenomena through weekly reports.

Science News® Keep up to date with the latest science discoveries.

Experience the complete textbook online and on CD-ROM.

Activities Practice skills and learn content.

Videos Explore content and learn important lab skills.

Audio Support Hear key terms spoken and defined.

Self-Assessment Use instant feedback to help you track your progress.

Activities

Researching the Problem

Do you recognize this invention by Lonnie Johnson?

Super Inventor

Engineer Lonnie Johnson was working on a new invention. He was experimenting with ways to cool the inside of a refrigerator with plain water instead of with harmful chemicals. As he tested his cooling system with a homemade nozzle in his bathroom sink, he noticed that he could blast a stream of water across the room. He stepped back and thought, "Wouldn't it be great if . . .?"

"That sink nozzle was the idea for a super squirter," says Lonnie. But to make a water gun that could store enough energy to shoot a stream of water forcefully, he had to solve an engineering problem. How could he get a high-pressure water stream from a toy that a child could operate? How could he make the water shoot out in almost the same way that water comes out of a fire hydrant?

Recently, Lonnie set up his own company. He invents new devices to solve tough problems in science and engineering. But he also puts his ideas to work to invent new toys and household products. Lonnie says that whether you're working on a space vehicle or a toy, the process of inventing is much the same.

Talking With
Lonnie Johnson

? What kind of kid were you?

I was always interested in how things work—in building and making things. My favorite toy was my erector set. I also liked those plastic building blocks. I used to take my brother's and sister's toys apart to see how they worked. And I used to repair stuff. If there was something broken around the house, like a lamp, I'd try to repair it. I learned from my father, too. He would work on his cars at home and that fascinated me. I was learning about machines by watching and helping him.

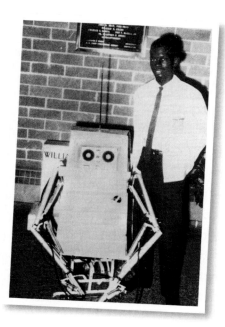

In high school, Lonnie won first place in a national science-fair competition with a homemade remote-control robot, which he called "Linex."

? How did you get interested in engineering?

The whole interest in building and fixing stuff—I guess that's where the seed came from. Repairing a broken lamp isn't all that different from inventing a super new toy. You need to be able to imagine how something works in your head, to see all the machine parts and how they'd work together—that's the basic skill. I'm usually pretty good at imagining how machines could be put together and work, whether they're big or small, simple or complex.

Career Path

Lonnie Johnson grew up in Alabama. He attended Tuskegee University and received a B.S. in mechanical engineering, an M.S. in nuclear engineering, and an honorary Ph.D. in science. He worked for the Jet Propulsion Laboratory in Pasadena, California. Now Lonnie owns his own company in Georgia.

❓ Do you solve problems all in your head? Or do you experiment?

I do both. It depends on the problem. Sometimes, just getting started is the key. You start building and putting things together, and other things reveal themselves along the way as you work.

For example, I have a long-term project I'm working on. I want to make a new kind of engine that's friendly to the environment, an engine that will make electricity from heat. In science, we call that a thermionic engine (from *therm,* the Greek root for "heat," and *ion,* an atom with an electrical charge). My first idea was a mechanical engine, one with moving parts. But we faced some real challenges when we tried to make it. So now I've got an engine idea that has no moving parts. I'm very excited about this particular solution. But I had to build the mechanical engine to realize that I needed to come up with a different engine.

❓ What happens if you get stuck?

When you have a problem you can't solve, you put it on hold. It sits there in the back of your mind. Then when you're doing something else, you find a clue.

I try to make that work in my company as well as inside my own head. We've got a toy side of the company that's very creative. The other side of the company is more hard science. We take the technology from the science side and use it in thinking up new toys. If you learn about how water works under pressure, you can invent a refrigerator, or a way to heat houses, or make a super squirt gun. There's a lot of crossing back and forth. I have a lot of fun.

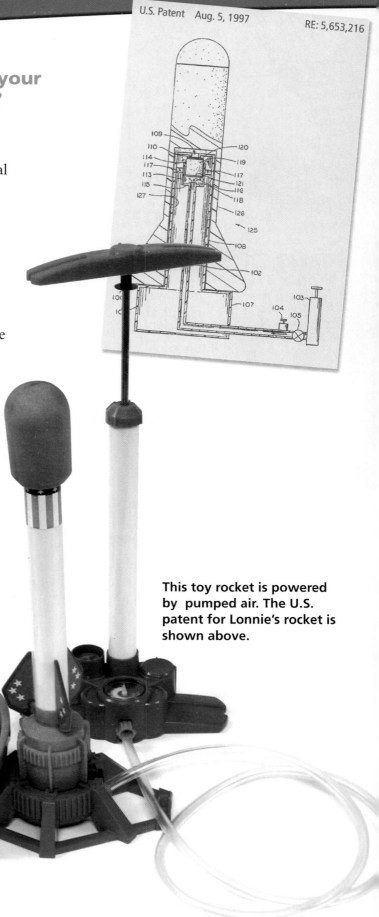

This toy rocket is powered by pumped air. The U.S. patent for Lonnie's rocket is shown above.

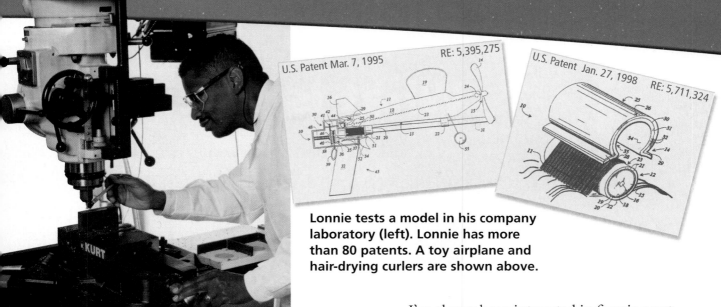

Lonnie tests a model in his company laboratory (left). Lonnie has more than 80 patents. A toy airplane and hair-drying curlers are shown above.

How do you get started on an invention?

You ask the question: What would be a great thing to have? You develop an overall idea. Then you define it by thinking of the specific problems that need to be solved.

Think about model rockets. I used to build model rockets when I was a kid. I'd order them through the mail, assemble them, and launch them. After a while, I made my own. I went to the library and found a book on how to build them. But those rockets used explosive chemicals for fuel. I wanted to make toy rockets that were cleaner and safer. So now I've invented rockets that use pumped air and water for power.

Is inventing hard?

If you can focus and work for a long time, you get very good at what you do. Problem solving is a process. There can be so many pieces to the puzzle. It's like a jigsaw puzzle. Sometimes all the pieces are there. Yet you can't even see them at first. But if you get your hands in and touch them and start working on it, you can start feeling the shapes. You start to understand how the pieces fit together.

I've always been interested in figuring out how to make things go and in working with new and different sources of power. When I was an engineer at NASA, I worked on the nuclear power source for the Galileo spacecraft. But I've also worked on powering toys with water and air, and making toy planes fly with rubber bands. The basic ideas are the same.

The trick is to keep working at it. Know what you're aiming for and keep looking for new solutions. Following through is also key to my philosophy: Believe in yourself and persevere. That's what I tell kids whenever I get the chance.

Writing in Science

Career Link Lonnie says the first step in an invention is the idea. Think of something that would be "a great thing to have," such as a toy or gadget. As an inventor, write a paragraph that describes your idea. Then, in a second paragraph, identify clearly some of the "little problems" you'll need to solve to make your idea work. (Remember, you don't need to know what the solutions will be.)

For: More on this career
Visit: PHSchool.com
Web Code: cgb-6000

Chapter

1

What Is Science?

*i*nteractive
Textbook

This food scientist is busy at ▶
work in a laboratory.

Discovery
CHANNEL
SCHOOL

What Is Science?

▶ **Video Preview**
Video Field Trip
Video Assessment

Lab zone™ Chapter **Project**

Is It Really True?

Is yawning contagious? Does a watched pot take longer to boil? When you drop a slice of bread, does it always land butter-side down? Questions like these are based on observations that people have made over the years. But are they true? In this chapter project, you will use scientific methods to find out.

Your Goal To design and conduct a scientific experiment to test whether a common belief is true or false

To complete this project, you must
● select one specific question to investigate
● identify the procedure you will follow to investigate your question
● collect data and use it to draw conclusions
● follow the safety guidelines in Appendix A

Plan It! Make a list of some common beliefs you could explore. Then preview the chapter to learn what types of questions can be explored by scientific methods. When you select a question, write the procedure you will follow. After your teacher approves your plan, begin your experiment.

Thinking Like a Scientist

Reading Preview

Key Concepts
- What skills do scientist use to learn about the world?
- What attitudes are important in science?

Key Terms
- observing
- quantitative observation
- qualitative observation
- inferring • predicting
- classifying • making models
- science • skepticism

Target Reading Skill

Asking Questions Before you read, preview the red headings. In a graphic organizer like the one below, ask a *what*, *how*, or *why* question for each heading. As you read, write answers to your questions.

Thinking Like a Scientist

Question	Answer
What does observing involve?	Observing involves . . .

For: More on scientific thinking
Visit: PHSchool.com
Web Code: cgd-6011

Discover **Activity**

How Keen Are Your Senses?

1. Your teacher has arranged for an unexpected event to occur. At the count of three, the event will begin.
2. List as many details as you can remember about the event.
3. Compare your list with those of your classmates.

Think It Over
Observing How many details could you list? Which of your senses did you use to gather information?

Once, as I walked through thick forest in a downpour, I suddenly saw a chimp hunched in front of me. Quickly I stopped. Then I heard a sound from above. I looked up and there was a big chimp there, too. When he saw me he gave a loud, clear wailing wraaaaah—a spine-chilling call that is used to threaten a dangerous animal. To my right I saw a large black hand shaking a branch and bright eyes glaring threateningly through the foliage. Then came another savage wraaaah from behind. Up above, the big male began to sway the vegetation. I was surrounded.

These words are from the writings of Jane Goodall, a scientist who studies wild chimpanzees in Gombe National Park in Tanzania, Africa. What would you have done if you were in Jane's shoes? Would you have screamed or tried to run away? Jane did neither of these things. Instead, she crouched down and stayed still so she wouldn't startle the chimps. Not feeling threatened by her, the chimps eventually moved on.

It is not always easy to study animals in their natural homes. But Jane was determined to learn all she could about these great apes. One of the most remarkable things about Jane Goodall is that she essentially trained herself to be a scientist. **Scientists use skills such as observing, inferring, predicting, classifying, and making models to learn more about the world.** However, these skills are not unique to scientists. You, too, think like a scientist every day.

Observing

Jane Goodall has spent countless hours among the chimpanzees—quietly following them, taking notes, and carefully observing. **Observing** means using one or more of your senses to gather information. Your senses include sight, hearing, touch, taste, and smell. By using her senses, Jane learned what chimpanzees eat, what sounds they make, and even what games they play! During her time in Gombe, Jane made many surprising observations. For example, she observed how chimpanzees use stems or long blades of grass as tools to "fish" out a tasty meal from termite mounds.

Like Jane, you use your senses to gather information. Look around you. What do you see? What do you hear and smell? You depend on your observations to help you make decisions throughout the day. For example, if it feels chilly when you wake up, you'll probably dress warmly.

Observations can be either quantitative or qualitative. **Quantitative observations** deal with a number, or amount. Seeing that you have eight new e-mails in your inbox is a quantitative observation. **Qualitative observations,** on the other hand, deal with descriptions that cannot be expressed in numbers. Noticing that a bike is blue or that a grape tastes sour are qualitative observations.

Figure 1
Observing
By patiently observing chimpanzees, Jane Goodall learned many things about chimpanzee behavior. The inset shows one of Jane's earliest discoveries—that chimps use sticks as tools to fish for termites.

 Reading Checkpoint **What senses can the skill of observation involve?**

Inferring

One day, Jane Goodall saw something peculiar. She watched as a chimpanzee peered into a hollow in a tree. The chimp picked off a handful of leaves from the tree and chewed on them. Then it took the leaves out of its mouth and pushed them into the tree hollow. When the chimp pulled the leaves back out, Jane saw the gleam of water. The chimp then put the wet leaves back in its mouth.

What was the chimpanzee doing? Jane reasoned that the chimpanzee might be using the chewed leaves like a sponge to soak up water. Seeing the chimp chew on leaves, put them in the hollow, and then squeeze the liquid out are all examples of observations. But Jane went beyond simply observing when she reasoned why the chimpanzee was doing these things. When you explain or interpret the things you observe, you are **inferring,** or making an inference.

Making an inference doesn't mean guessing wildly. Inferences are based on reasoning from what you already know. Jane knew that chimpanzees, like all other animals, need water, and that rainwater collects in tree hollows. She reasoned that the chimp was using chewed leaves to get the water out of the tree.

You, too, make inferences all the time. Because your brain processes observations and other information so quickly, you may not even realize when you have made an inference. For example, if you see your friend smile after getting back an exam, you might automatically infer that she got a good grade. Inferences are not always correct, however. Your friend's smile might not have anything to do with the test.

Reading Checkpoint What is inferring?

FIGURE 2
Inferring
When you explain or interpret your observations, you are making an inference. **Inferring** *List three inferences you can make about this chimp.*

Predicting

Jane's understanding of chimpanzee behavior grew as time went by. Sometimes, she could even predict what a chimp was going to do next. **Predicting** means making a forecast of what will happen in the future based on past experience or evidence.

Through her observations, Jane learned that when a chimpanzee is frightened or angry, its hairs stand on end. This response is sometimes followed by threatening gestures such as charging, throwing rocks, and shaking trees, or even an attack. Therefore, if Jane sees a chimp with its hairs on end, she can predict that there might be danger and move away.

Likewise, you would probably move away if you saw a dog growling or baring its teeth. Why? Because predicting is part of your everyday thinking. You might predict, for example, that your basketball team will win tonight's game if you have always beaten the other team in the past. Predictions, of course, are not always correct. New players this year may increase the other team's chances of winning.

Predictions and inferences are closely related. While inferences are attempts to explain what is happening or *has* happened, predictions are forecasts of what *will* happen. If you see a broken egg on the floor by a table, you might infer that the egg had rolled off the table. If, however, you see an egg rolling toward the edge of a table, you can predict that it's about to create a mess.

FIGURE 3
Predicting
Predictions are forecasts of what will happen next.
Predicting *What do you think this chimp will do next?*

 **Reading Checkpoint** **What are predictions based on?**

Math Analyzing Data

Chimp Food

This graph shows the diet of chimps at Gombe National Park during May of one year.

1. **Reading Graphs** According to the graph, what foods do chimps eat?

2. **Interpreting Data** Did chimps feed more on seeds or leaves during this month?

3. **Calculating** What percentage of the diet did blossoms, seeds, leaves, and fruit make up?

4. **Predicting** Suppose you learn that November is the main termite-fishing season, when chimps spend a large part of their time eating termites. Predict how the chimp diet might change in November.

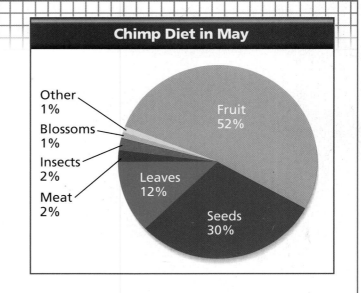

Chimp Diet in May

Other 1%
Blossoms 1%
Insects 2%
Meat 2%
Fruit 52%
Leaves 12%
Seeds 30%

Resting

FIGURE 4
Classifying
Field notes like these contain many details about a chimp's daily activities. By grouping together all the information related to resting, climbing, or feeding, Jane can better understand the chimp's behavior.

6:45 Jomeo in nest

6:50 Jomeo leaves nest, climbs, feeds on *viazi pori* fruit

7:16 Wanders along, feeding on *budyankende* fruits

8:08 Stops feeding, climbs, and feeds on *viazi pori* fruit again

8:35 Travels

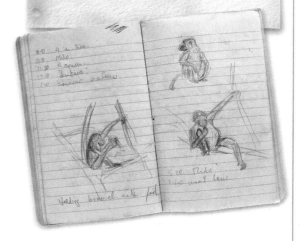

Classifying

What do chimps do all day? To find out, Jane and her assistants followed the chimpanzees through the forest. They took detailed field notes about the chimps' behaviors. Figure 4 shows a short section of notes about Jomeo, an adult male chimp.

Suppose Jane wanted to know how much time Jomeo spent feeding or resting that morning. She could find out by classifying Jomeo's actions into several categories. **Classifying** is the process of grouping together items that are alike in some way. For example, Jane could group together all the information about Jomeo's feeding habits or his resting behavior. This would also make it easier to compare Jomeo's actions to those of other chimps. For instance, she could determine if other adult males feed or rest as much as Jomeo does.

You, too, classify objects and information all the time. Classifying things helps you to stay organized so you can easily find and use them later. When you put papers in a notebook, you might classify them by subject or date. And, you might have one drawer in your dresser for shirts and another for socks.

 Reading Checkpoint **How is classifying objects useful?**

Climbing

Feeding

Making Models

How far do chimpanzees travel? Where do they go? Sometimes, Jane's research team would follow a particular chimpanzee for many days at a time. Figure 5 illustrates Jomeo's journey through the forest over the course of one day. The diagram is one example of a model. **Making models** involves creating representations of complex objects or processes. Models help people study and understand things that are complex or that can't be observed directly. Using a model like the one in Figure 5, Jane and her assistants could share information that would otherwise be difficult to explain.

Models are all around you. They include physical objects, such as globes and movie sets used in filming your favorite TV show. Some models are generated by computer, like the ones some architects use to design new buildings. It's important to keep in mind that models are only representations of the real object or process. Because some information may be missing from a model, you may not be able to understand everything about the object or process the model represents.

 **Reading Checkpoint** **What is a model?**

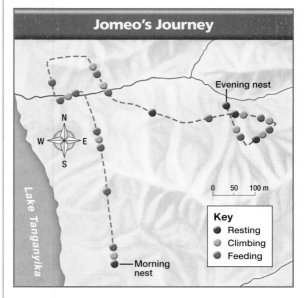

FIGURE 5
Making Models
This map is a model that traces Jomeo's journey through the forest. It represents information that would be hard to explain in words. **Interpreting Maps** *What is the total distance that Jomeo traveled between the morning and evening nests?*

Scientific Attitudes

Why has Jane Goodall devoted her life to studying chimps? Some people might say that she wants to contribute to "science." **Science** is a way of learning about the natural world. Science also includes all of the knowledge gained by exploring the natural world. **Successful scientists possess certain important attitudes, or habits of mind, including curiosity, honesty, open-mindedness, skepticism, and creativity.**

Curiosity An important attitude that drives scientists is curiosity. Successful scientists are eager to learn more about the topics they study. They stick with problems in spite of setbacks.

Honesty Good scientists always report their observations and results truthfully. Honesty is especially important when a scientist's results go against previous ideas or predictions.

Open-Mindedness and Skepticism Scientists need to be open-minded, or capable of accepting new and different ideas. However, open-mindedness should always be balanced by **skepticism,** which is having an attitude of doubt.

Creativity Whether scientists study chimps or earthquakes, problems may arise in their studies. Sometimes, it takes a bit of creativity to find a solution. Creativity means coming up with inventive ways to solve problems or produce new things.

 **Reading Checkpoint** What is skepticism?

FIGURE 6
Curiosity
Scientists are driven by a curiosity to learn more about what they are studying. This scientist is recording bird calls in a rain forest in Costa Rica.

Section 1 Assessment

Target Reading Skill Asking Questions Use the answers to the questions you wrote about the headings to help you answer the questions below.

Reviewing Key Concepts

1. **a.** Listing Name five skills that are important in scientific thinking.
   b. Comparing and Contrasting How do observations differ from inferences?
   c. Classifying Is this statement an observation or an inference? *The cat must be ill.* Explain your reasoning.
2. **a.** Identifying What attitudes help scientists succeed in their work?
   b. Explaining Why is it important for scientists to balance open-mindedness and skepticism?
   c. Making Judgments Is it important to be both open-minded and skeptical in your everyday life? Explain.

Lab zone At-Home **Activity**

"Pastabilities" Collect pasta of various shapes and sizes. You and a family member should each devise a system to classify the pasta into three groups. How similar were your groupings?

Scientific Inquiry

Reading Preview

Key Concepts
- What is scientific inquiry?
- What makes a hypothesis testable?
- How do scientific theories differ from scientific laws?

Key Terms
- scientific inquiry
- hypothesis • variable
- manipulated variable
- responding variable
- controlled experiment
- operational definition • data
- communicating
- scientific theory • scientific law

Target Reading Skill

Building Vocabulary A definition states the meaning of a word or phrase by telling about its most important feature or function. After you read this section, reread the paragraphs that contain definitions of Key Terms. Use all the information you have learned to write a definition of each Key Term in your own words.

▼ A snowy tree cricket

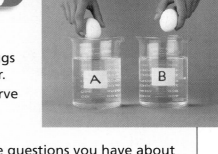

Lab zone Discover **Activity**

What's Happening?
1. Your teacher will give you two eggs and two beakers filled with water.
2. Put one egg in each beaker. Observe what happens.

Think It Over
Posing Questions Write down three questions you have about your observations. How could you find out the answer?

"Chirp, chirp, chirp." It is one of the hottest nights of summer and your bedroom windows are wide open. On most nights, the quiet chirping of crickets gently lulls you to sleep, but not tonight. The noise from the crickets is almost deafening. "Chirp, chirp, chirp, chirp, chirp!"

Why do all the crickets in your neighborhood seem determined to keep you awake tonight? Could the crickets be chirping more because of the heat? How could you find out?

As you lie awake, you are probably not thinking much about science. But, in fact, you are thinking just as a scientist would. You made observations—you heard the loud chirping of the crickets and felt the heat of the summer night. Your observations led you to infer that heat might cause increased chirping. You might even make a prediction: "If it's cooler tomorrow night, the crickets will be quieter, and I can get a good night's sleep!"

Although you might not know it, your thinking and questioning is the start of the **scientific inquiry** process. **Scientific inquiry refers to the diverse ways in which scientists study the natural world and propose explanations based on the evidence they gather.** If you have ever tried to figure out why your CD player has stopped working, then you have used scientific inquiry. Similarly, you could use scientific inquiry to find out whether there is a relationship between the air temperature and crickets' chirping.

Posing Questions

Scientific inquiry often begins with a problem or question about an observation. In the case of the crickets, your question might be: Does the air temperature affect the chirping of crickets? Of course, questions don't just come to you from nowhere. Instead, questions come from experiences that you have and from observations and inferences that you make. Curiosity plays a large role as well. Think of a time that you observed something unusual or unexpected. Chances are good that your curiosity sparked a number of questions.

Some questions cannot be investigated by scientific inquiry. Think about the difference between the two questions below.

- Why has my CD player stopped working?

- What kind of music should I listen to on my CD player?

The first question is a scientific question because it can be answered by making observations and gathering evidence. For example, you could change the batteries in your CD player and observe whether it begins to work. In contrast, the second question has to do with personal opinions or values. Scientific inquiry cannot answer questions about personal tastes or judgments.

Reading Checkpoint What role does curiosity play in posing questions?

FIGURE 7
Posing Questions
Scientific inquiry often begins with a problem or question. Questions often arise from experiences or observations.

The temperature is really warm tonight.

I wonder if the air temperature affects the chirping of crickets.

Developing a Hypothesis

How could you explain your observation of noisy crickets on that summer night? "Perhaps crickets chirp more when the temperature is higher," you think. In trying to answer the question, you are in fact developing a hypothesis. A **hypothesis** (plural: *hypotheses*) is a possible explanation for a set of observations or answer to a scientific question. In this case, your hypothesis would be that cricket chirping increases at higher air temperatures.

It is important to realize that a hypothesis is *not* a fact. Instead, it is only one possible way to explain a group of observations. In the case of the crickets, perhaps they only sounded louder that night because you had left more windows open than you usually do. Or, maybe there were more crickets around that night.

In science, a hypothesis must be testable. This means that researchers must be able to carry out investigations and gather evidence that will either support or disprove the hypothesis. Many trials will be needed before a hypothesis can be accepted as true.

 **What is a hypothesis?**

What Is Science?

Video Preview
▶ Video Field Trip
Video Assessment

> Perhaps crickets chirp more when the temperature is higher.

FIGURE 8
Developing Hypotheses
A hypothesis is one possible way to explain a set of observations. A hypothesis must be testable— scientists must be able to carry out investigations to test the hypothesis.
Developing Hypotheses *Propose another hypothesis that could account for this boy's observations.*

Designing an Experiment

After you state your hypothesis, you are ready to design an experiment to test it. You know that your experiment will involve counting how many times crickets chirp when the air temperature is high. But how will you know how many times the crickets would chirp at a lower temperature? You would need to include other crickets in your experiment for comparison.

Controlling Variables To test your hypothesis, then, you will need to observe crickets at different air temperatures. All other **variables,** or factors that can change in an experiment, must be exactly the same. Other variables include the kind of crickets, the type of container you test them in, and the type of thermometer. By keeping all of these variables the same, you will know that any difference in cricket chirping must be due to temperature alone.

The one variable that is purposely changed to test a hypothesis is called the **manipulated variable** (also called the independent variable). In your cricket experiment, the manipulated variable is the air temperature. The factor that may change in response to the manipulated variable is called the **responding variable** (also called the dependent variable). The responding variable here is the number of cricket chirps.

We've set up the containers to be identical except for the temperature conditions.

Now we have to agree on how to time and count the chirps.

15°C

20°C

CRICKETS

Setting Up a Controlled Experiment An experiment in which only one variable is manipulated at a time is called a **controlled experiment.** Figure 9 shows one way to set up a controlled experiment to test your cricket hypothesis. Notice that identical containers, thermometers, leaves, and crickets are used in each setup. In one container, the temperature will be maintained at 15°C. In the other two containers, the temperatures will be kept at 20°C and 25°C.

The Importance of Controlling Variables Suppose you decide to test the crickets at 15°C in the morning and the crickets at 20°C and 25°C in the afternoon. Is this a controlled experiment? The answer is no. Your experiment would have two variables—temperature and time of day. Would increased chirping be due to the temperature difference? Or are crickets more active at certain times of day? There would be no way to know which variable explained your results.

Forming Operational Definitions One other important aspect of a well-designed experiment is having clear operational definitions. An **operational definition** is a statement that describes how to measure a particular variable or define a particular term. For example, in this experiment you would need to determine what sounds will count as a single "chirp."

 **Reading Checkpoint** **What is a manipulated variable?**

FIGURE 9
A Controlled Experiment
In their controlled experiment, these students are using the same kind of containers, thermometers, leaves, and crickets. The manipulated variable in this experiment is temperature. The responding variable is the number of cricket chirps per minute at each temperature.
Controlling Variables *What other variables must the students keep constant in this experiment?*

Collecting and Interpreting Data

You are almost ready to begin your experiment. But first, you must decide how many crickets to test. Because individual differences exist from cricket to cricket, you will need to test more than just one or two. You decide to test five crickets at each temperature.

Organizing Your Data Before you begin your experiment, you should create a table like the one in Figure 10 in which to record your data. **Data** are the facts, figures, and other evidence gathered through observations. A data table provides you with an organized way to collect and record your observations.

Graphing Your Results After all the data have been collected, they need to be interpreted. One useful tool that can help you interpret data is a graph. Graphs will be discussed in more detail in Chapter 2.

Study the graph in Figure 10 to see how graphing can help you make sense of your data. Graphs can reveal patterns or trends in data. For example, notice that your data points seem to fall in a line. You can see that as the temperature increases from 15°C to 25°C, the number of chirps per minute also increases.

 **Reading Checkpoint** What are data?

FIGURE 10
Collecting and Interpreting Data
A data table helps you organize the information you collect in an experiment. Graphing the data may reveal any patterns in your data.
Interpreting Data Did all of the crickets chirp more at 25°C than at 20°C? Did you use the data table or the graph to answer this question?

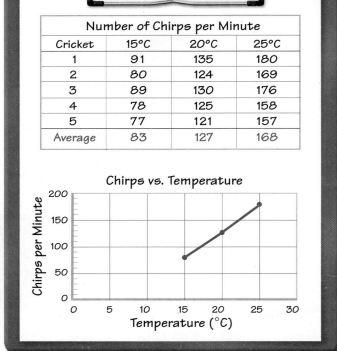

Number of Chirps per Minute

Cricket	15°C	20°C	25°C
1	91	135	180
2	80	124	169
3	89	130	176
4	78	125	158
5	77	121	157
Average	83	127	168

Chirps vs. Temperature

Drawing Conclusions

Now that you have gathered and interpreted your data, you can draw conclusions about your hypothesis. A conclusion is a summary of what you have learned from an experiment. In drawing your conclusion, you should ask yourself whether the data supports the hypothesis. You also need to consider whether you collected enough data and whether anything happened during the experiment that might have affected the results. You should address these questions in your summary of the experiment.

After reviewing the data, you decide that the evidence supports your original hypothesis. You conclude that cricket chirping does increase with temperature. It's no wonder that you have trouble sleeping on those warm summer nights!

Inquiry Leads to Inquiry Scientific inquiry usually doesn't end once a set of experiments is done. Often, one scientific inquiry leads into another one. You have found that crickets do indeed chirp more as the temperature rises. But does this apply to all kinds of crickets everywhere? And what happens at lower temperatures? These new questions can lead to new hypotheses and new experiments.

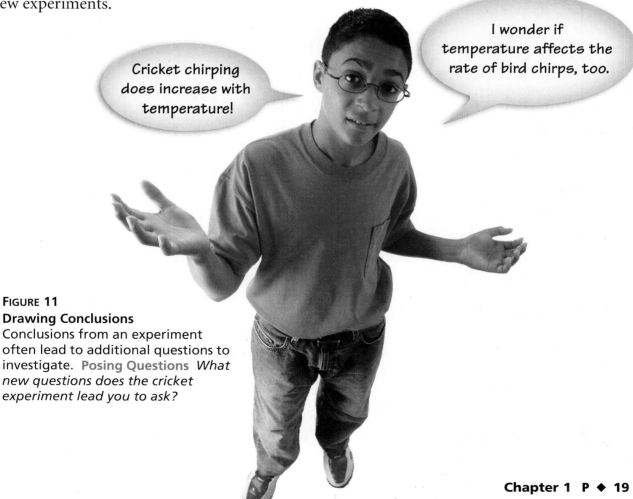

Cricket chirping does increase with temperature!

I wonder if temperature affects the rate of bird chirps, too.

FIGURE 11
Drawing Conclusions
Conclusions from an experiment often lead to additional questions to investigate. Posing Questions *What new questions does the cricket experiment lead you to ask?*

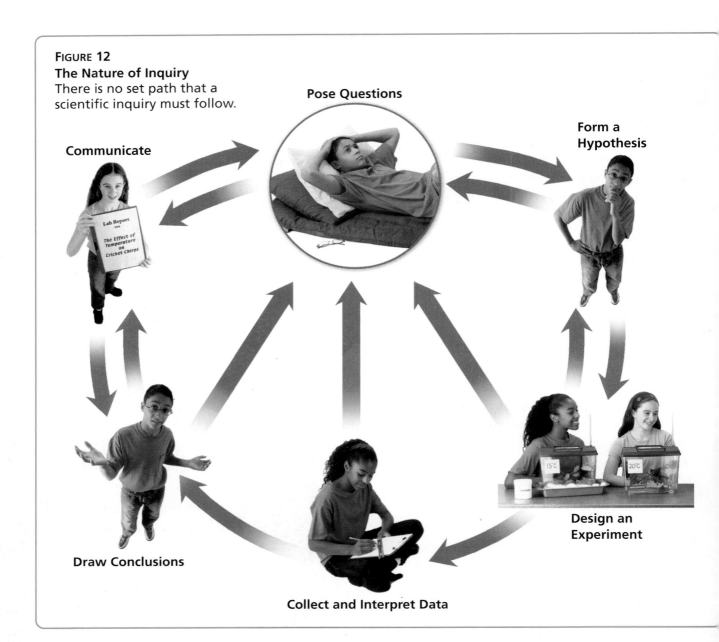

FIGURE 12
The Nature of Inquiry
There is no set path that a scientific inquiry must follow.

Pose Questions

Form a Hypothesis

Communicate

Lab Report
***
The Effect of Temperature on Cricket Chirps

Design an Experiment

15℃   20℃

Draw Conclusions

Collect and Interpret Data

The Nature of Inquiry In this cricket experiment, you decided to test your hypothesis in one particular way. Your friend may do it another way. Furthermore, different questions may require different approaches to finding answers. For example, a scientist studying the moon may rely more on observations rather than controlled experiments to test a hypothesis.

Scientific inquiry is a process with many paths, not a rigid sequence of steps. Often, a surprising observation or accidental discovery leads into inquiry. New information springs up, then a scientist's path takes a different turn. Work may go forward—or even backward—when testing a hunch or fitting a new idea with existing ones.

Communicating

An important part of the scientific inquiry process is communicating your results. **Communicating** is the sharing of ideas and experimental findings with others through writing and speaking. Scientists share their ideas in many ways. For example, they give talks at scientific meetings, exchange information on the Internet, or publish articles in scientific journals.

Sometimes, a scientific inquiry can be part of a huge project with many scientists working together around the world. On such projects, scientists must share their ideas and findings on a regular basis. When scientists communicate their research, they describe their procedures in full detail so that others can repeat their experiments.

 **Reading Checkpoint** **Why is communicating important to scientists?**

Scientific Theories and Laws

As a body of knowledge, science is built up cautiously. Scientists do not accept a new hypothesis after just one successful experiment. Rather, a hypothesis is tested repeatedly as many different scientists try to apply it to their own work.

Scientific Theories Sometimes, a large set of related observations can be connected by a single explanation. This can lead to the development of a scientific theory. A **scientific theory** is a well-tested explanation for a wide range of observations or experimental results. For example, according to the atomic theory, all substances are composed of tiny particles called atoms. The atomic theory helps to explain many observations, such as why ice melts at a particular temperature and why iron nails rust.

Scientists accept a theory only when there is a large body of evidence that supports it. However, future testing can still prove an accepted theory to be incorrect. If that happens, scientists may modify the theory, or discard it altogether. This illustrates the ever growing—and exciting—nature of scientific knowledge.

FIGURE **13**
A Scientific Theory
Based on observations of sunsets and sunrises, ancient people theorized that the sun revolved around Earth. New evidence led scientists to abandon that ancient theory. Today, scientists know that Earth, along with the other planets in the solar system, revolves around the sun.

FIGURE 14
A Scientific Law
According to the law of gravity, this parachutist will eventually land back on Earth.

Scientific Laws Have you ever heard someone say, "What goes up must come down"? When scientists repeatedly observe the same result in specific circumstances, they may arrive at a scientific law. A **scientific law** is a statement that describes what scientists expect to happen every time under a particular set of conditions.

Unlike a theory, a scientific law describes an observed pattern in nature without attempting to explain it. You can think of a scientific law as a rule of nature. For example, the law of gravity states that all objects in the universe attract each other. This law has been verified over and over again.

 **Reading Checkpoint** **What does a scientific law describe?**

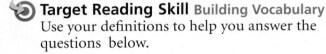

Section 2 Assessment

Target Reading Skill Building Vocabulary Use your definitions to help you answer the questions below.

Reviewing Key Concepts

1. a. Defining Define the term *scientific inquiry*.
  b. Explaining A friend claims that ceiling fans are better than air conditioning because they cool the air faster than air conditioners do. Could you investigate this through scientific inquiry? Explain.
  c. Problem Solving What kind of data would you need to collect to carry out this experiment?

2. a. Reviewing What is meant by saying that a hypothesis must be testable?
  b. Developing Hypotheses Every time you and your friend study for an exam while listening to classical music, both of you do well on the exam. What testable hypothesis can you develop from your observations?

3. a. Defining What is a scientific theory? What is a scientific law?
  b. Comparing and Contrasting How do scientific theories differ from scientific laws?
  c. Classifying The students who conducted the cricket experiment concluded that their results supported their hypothesis. Can their supported hypothesis be called a theory? Why or why not?

Writing in Science

Summary Suppose you will be traveling to a convention of cricket scientists from around the world. Write a paragraph describing the results of your cricket experiment. Include questions you'd like to ask other cricket scientists while at the conference.

Keeping Flowers Fresh

Problem

How can cut flowers stay fresher for a longer period of time?

Skills Focus

developing hypotheses, designing experiments, drawing conclusions

Suggested Materials

• plastic cups   • cut flowers   • spoon   • water
• sugar

Design a Plan

1. You have just been given a bouquet of cut flowers. You remember once seeing a gardener put some sugar into the water in a vase before putting flowers in. You wonder if the gardener did that so that the flowers would stay fresh longer. Write a hypothesis for an experiment you could perform to answer your question.

2. Working with a partner, design a controlled experiment to test your hypothesis. Make a list of all of the variables you will need to control. Also decide what data you will need to collect. For example, you could count the number of petals each flower drops. Then write out a detailed experimental plan for your teacher to review.

3. If necessary, revise your plan according to your teacher's instructions. Then set up your experiment and begin collecting your data.

Analyze and Conclude

1. **Developing Hypotheses** What hypothesis did you decide to test? On what information or experience was your hypothesis based?

2. **Designing Experiments** What was the manipulated variable in the experiment you performed? What was the responding variable? What variables were kept constant?

3. **Graphing** Use the data you collected to create one or more graphs of your experimental results. (For more on creating graphs, see the Skills Handbook.) What patterns or trends do your graphs reveal?

4. **Drawing Conclusions** Based on your graphs, what conclusion can you draw about sugar and cut flowers? Do your results support your hypothesis? Why or why not?

5. **Communicating** In a paragraph, describe which aspects of your experimental plan were difficult to carry out. Were any variables hard to control? Was it difficult to collect accurate data? What changes could you make to improve your experimental plan?

More to Explore

Make a list of some additional questions you would like to investigate about how to keep cut flowers fresh. Choose one of the questions and write a hypothesis for an experiment you could perform. Then design a controlled experiment to test your hypothesis. *Obtain your teacher's permission before carrying out your investigation.*

Why Study Science?

Reading Preview

Key Concepts
- Why do people need to understand scientific principles and think scientifically?
- What is scientific literacy and why is it important?

Key Term
- scientific literacy

Target Reading Skill
Identifying Main Ideas As you read about the importance of studying science, write the main idea in a graphic organizer like the one below. Then write four supporting details that further explain the idea.

Main Idea

Understanding science can help you . . .

Detail	Detail	Detail	Detail

Lab zone Discover **Activity**

How Much Do You See or Hear About Science?

1. Watch a half-hour evening news broadcast. List all the news stories that have something to do with a science topic.
2. Watch the ads during the broadcast and list the ones that make scientific claims.

Think It Over
Inferring Were you surprised at how often science topics were mentioned on the news or in ads? Based on your observations, why is it important to study science?

Your eyes are glued to the screen. You watch as two explorers from the special investigations unit, Theta 7, activate the matter resequencer and teleport to their next destination. Three thousandths of a second later, they arrive at Sector 1572. The land is inhabited by giant fire ants and other creatures grown out of proportion. Because the explorers' garments make them nearly invisible, they move through the sector without being noticed by the giant creatures.

As the movie ends, you think how great it would be if you could teleport yourself or become invisible. This was only a movie, but could these things be possible some day? What about the giant ants? Could insects that large ever really exist?

From science fiction movies to nightly news reports, science is all around you. That's why you need to have a basic knowledge of science. **Being able to understand scientific principles and think scientifically can help you solve problems and answer many questions in your everyday life.** This section presents some of the questions that people ask every day.

How Does It Work?

You are standing in line at the grocery store. The cashier scans each item with a laser. The customer in front of you pulls out a credit card and runs the magnetic stripe through a slot. The machine reads information on the card and sends the data to a distant computer. Devices such as these are a common part of our daily lives. They have changed almost every aspect of how people live and work. All of them have some basis in science. But could you explain how any of these devices work?

Of course, as a customer, you don't really need to know how these devices work. But what if you were the cashier and one of the devices stopped working? Or what if you were shopping for a bicycle? Do you know how gears work or which metal is lightweight, yet sturdy? Knowing some science and thinking scientifically could help you make the right choice.

Learning science can also help you understand natural events that affect your daily life. For example, how do tornadoes form? Can listening to loud music damage your hearing? Being able to answer questions like these can help you make wise decisions and stay safe.

 **How might knowing science help you shop for a bicycle?**

FIGURE 15
How Things Work
Learning the science behind how things work can help make everyday activities, such as biking, safer and more enjoyable.
Posing Questions *What other bike-related questions do you have?*

What materials are helmets made of? How do they protect your head?

How do different types of brakes work? How quickly can you come to a stop?

How do gears work? How many gears do you need for the biking you plan to do?

FIGURE 16
Staying Healthy
Knowing the science behind health and nutrition issues can help you make wise shopping decisions.
Making Judgments What scientific information do you rely on when making food choices?

How Can I Stay Healthy?

"Jump higher, run faster! Improve your athletic abilities with new Superstar Energy Bar. Buy it now!" This is not a real advertisement, but you may have seen ads with similar claims. Would you buy the product based on this ad? If not, suppose the ad went on to say, "Studies have shown that Superstar Energy Bar improves people's athletic abilities more than other brands." Now would you be convinced?

Scientific thinking can help you to evaluate advertised claims. For example, you might question whether the claims are based on a controlled study. You might want to know how the study measured improvement in athletic ability and how many people were studied.

Eating well is one way to maintain your health. Getting enough exercise and avoiding exposure to disease are other ways. Which exercises are best for you? Should you take pills to help your muscles grow stronger? Can going out on a cold, wet day really make you sick? These are the kinds of questions that studying science will help you answer.

 **Reading Checkpoint** **What information might help you evaluate advertised claims?**

How Do I Become an Informed Citizen?

Have you ever heard people discuss their views on a public issue? For example, should a town restrict water use in the summer? Should scientists continue to explore space? Should old paint in a building be removed? Issues like these often generate much debate.

Take space exploration, for example. What can we learn from space missions? What are the costs and risks? Would the money be better spent on projects closer to home? These are just a few of the questions that might come up during a debate.

As you grow older, you will have more and more opportunities to voice your opinion on public issues—at public hearings, in the voting booth, or by just talking with friends. And more and more public issues involve science. Understanding the science will help you weigh the pros and cons and arrive at a decision.

Reading Checkpoint **Where are some places you can voice your opinions on public issues?**

What Is the Best Use of Earth's Resources?

"Paper or plastic?" Have you ever heard this question from a store clerk? Although the question seems simple, it's not. Do you know enough science to arrive at an answer?

You might be surprised to learn that the clerk's question has something to do with science. But think about how these bags were produced and where they might end up after you use them. Is one choice better than the other? That is a complex question that scientists are studying.

Scientists are also studying other topics related to Earth's resources. For example, you may have heard about cars that run on fuels other than gasoline. What are the advantages and disadvantages of these types of cars? What's involved in developing other sources of fuels?

Topics related to Earth's resources may seem far removed from your life, but in fact, they're not. Have you ever wondered where the water in your toilet comes from? Where does the water go after you flush the toilet? And why do adults always tell you to turn off the lights when you leave a room? Could the world's energy sources ever really run out? Learning science will help you answer questions like these.

 **Reading Checkpoint** What are two decisions related to Earth's resources that you faced today?

FIGURE 17
Using Earth's Resources Wisely
Should you walk or ride in a car to a nearby destination? Knowing science can help you make wise decisions that impact Earth's resources.

What materials make the best support for a roller coaster? What kind of ground should a roller coaster be built on?

FIGURE 18
Scientific Literacy
Even a roller coaster ride can generate many scientific questions! Having scientific literacy can help you identify good sources of scientific information in which to find answers.

For: Links on scientific literacy
Visit: www.SciLinks.org
Web Code: scn-1613

Scientific Literacy

Are you still wondering why you should study science? Or, at this point, are you instead wondering how you could possibly learn everything there is to know?

Of course, it is not possible to become an expert in every field of science. Nor is it possible to test everything scientifically by yourself. Instead, you need to have scientific literacy. Having **scientific literacy** means that you understand basic scientific terms and principles well enough that you can evaluate information, make personal decisions, and take part in public affairs. **By having scientific literacy, you will be able to identify good sources of scientific information, evaluate them for accuracy, and apply the knowledge to questions or problems in your life.** You will also be able to keep up with the latest scientific trends and be well qualified for jobs.

So, why should you study science? The real question is, why wouldn't you?

Why is a good understanding of scientific terms and principles important?

Why don't roller coasters fall off the track when they go upside down?

What causes that feeling of queasiness or exhilaration?

Section 3 Assessment

Target Reading Skill

Identifying Main Ideas Use your graphic organizer about the importance of studying science to answer the questions below.

Reviewing Key Concepts

1. a. **Reviewing** List two questions that a knowledge of science could help you answer.
   b. **Summarizing** How does understanding scientific principles and thinking scientifically apply to your everyday life?
   c. **Applying Concepts** A friend tells you that studying science is only for scientists. How could you convince your friend otherwise?

2. a. **Defining** What is scientific literacy?
   b. **Problem Solving** You are watching the news on TV and hear about "DNA fingerprinting." How could you find out what that is?

Writing in Science

Comic Strip Design a five-panel comic strip that illustrates the importance of science education in a humorous way. Your comic strip should show a particular situation in which a knowledge of science would have been important.

Careers in Science

Reading Preview

Key Concepts
- What are the three main branches of science?
- Why is important for scientists in different fields to work together?
- How is science important in nonscience careers?

Target Reading Skill

Using Prior Knowledge Before you read, look at the section headings and visuals to see what this section is about. Then write what you know about scientists in a graphic organizer like the one below. As you read, continue to write in what you learn.

What You Know
1. There are different fields of science.
2.

What You Learned
1.
2.

Lab zone Discover Activity

What Do Scientists Look Like?

1. On a sheet of paper, draw a picture of a scientist at work.
2. Compare your picture to that of a classmate.
3. Use both of your pictures to list the characteristics of a "typical" scientist.

Think it Over
Inferring Where do you think your ideas about typical scientists come from?

How would you like to live and work on an island? Can you work under challenging conditions, such as extreme heat? Would you like to hike and explore new places? Would you enjoy flying in helicopters? If you answered yes to these questions, maybe you should consider becoming a scientist!

This job description probably doesn't match your idea of what a scientist does. But it accurately describes the work of a volcanologist, a scientist who studies volcanoes. Volcanologists do such things as collect and study samples of molten rock after a volcano has erupted. Other scientists can be found at work in the oceans, in laboratories, on glaciers, and in outer space. Wherever people are asking questions and searching for answers, they are using the skills of scientific inquiry.

Earth science:
Volcanologist

Branches of Science

How many different science careers can you name? Your list would probably include such careers as astronauts, doctors, and engineers. But would it also include crystallographers—scientists who study the three-dimensional structure of chemicals? How about ornithologists—scientists who study birds? As you can see, the term *scientist* spans many diverse fields and interests.

Because the areas of scientific study are so diverse, scientists organize their work into three major branches, or fields of study. **The three main branches of science are earth and space science, physical science, and life science.**

Earth and Space Science Earth and space science is the study of Earth and its place in the universe. Some earth scientists study the forces that have shaped Earth throughout its long history. Others study Earth's oceans or its weather. Space scientists study the planets and stars that exist beyond Earth.

Physical Science Physical science includes the study of energy, motion, sound, light, electricity, and magnetism. It also includes chemistry—the study of the tiny particles that make up all things, from flowers to stars.

Life Science Life science is the study of living things, including plants, animals, and microscopic life forms. Life scientists also study how living things interact with each other and with their surroundings. The study of the human body is part of life sciences, too.

Reading Checkpoint **What topics of study does physical science include?**

FIGURE 19
Branches of Science

The diverse topics of scientific study can be classified into three main branches: earth and space science, physical science, and life science. **Classifying** *Which branch of science includes the study of clouds?*

Physical science:
Chemist

Life science:
Ornithologists

For: Links on branches of science
Visit: www.SciLinks.org
Web Code: scn-1614

Scientists Working Together

Although it is convenient to think of science as divided into three branches, these areas are not really separate at all. Most scientific questions being investigated today span the different fields of science.

If you have ever worked on a difficult jigsaw puzzle with friends, then you can understand how scientists study questions and solve problems. One friend might work on one corner of the puzzle, while you work on another. Similarly, a physical scientist might investigate one piece of a scientific "puzzle" while an earth scientist works on another piece of the same puzzle. As you read about two scientific questions being investigated today, you can see how they involve the cooperation of a wide range of scientists.

Exploring Beyond Earth Will it someday be possible for humans to live in space? The International Space Station was designed in part to study this question. In orbit since 1998, the space station has been home to many crews, who stay for months at a time. On board, scientists explore the challenges of living in space. On the ground, hundreds of other scientists make the work of the crew possible.

 **Reading Checkpoint** How is scientific inquiry similar to assembling a jigsaw puzzle?

FIGURE 20
The International Space Station
The International Space Station continually travels around Earth, about 400 km above the ground. *Posing Questions What questions are the scientists who work on the space station trying to answer?*

FIGURE 21
Exploring Space
It takes the work of many scientists to address the challenges of living in space.

Astronauts
Some astronauts pilot the space station, while others carry out experiments. They may study how living in space affects muscle strength or whether crops can be grown in space.

Computer Scientists
On Earth, computer scientists design programs that manage many aspects of space flight, from keeping the temperature stable to controlling the space station's robotic arm.

Food Scientists
Eating in space is a challenge. Food scientists develop foods for space flights that are easy to use, nutritious, and, perhaps most importantly, tasty!

Materials Scientists
Materials scientists study the properties of materials such as ceramics to understand how they would perform in the harsh environment of space.

A soybean-powered bus ▲

Developing a New Source of Energy Imagine boarding a bus that didn't run on gasoline—but on soybeans instead! Buses like these already exist in several cities. Fuels made from soybeans or other plant matter are called biofuels. Unlike gasoline and oil, biofuels burn cleaner and are readily available.

What kinds of plants make good fuels? What conditions do they need to grow? And how can the energy in plants be converted into fuels? These are questions that botanists, soil scientists, chemists, and many other scientists are working together to answer. The goal of all these scientists is to produce high-quality, inexpensive biofuels that do not contaminate, or pollute, the environment.

 **Reading Checkpoint** **What are biofuels?**

FIGURE 22
Developing Biofuels

Many scientists are studying biofuels as a promising new source of energy.
Predicting *What problems might arise if the scientists on this project didn't communicate with one another?*

Botanists
Fuel crops must be easy to plant, grow, and process. Botanists, or plant biologists, are studying soybeans, corn, trees, and fast-growing grasses as potential fuel crops.

Soil Scientists
Soil scientists provide information about soil conditions. They help identify crops that may be used for both producing fuel and for improving the soil.

Chemists
To obtain the best fuels, chemists analyze the chemical makeup in plants and experiment with various methods of producing fuels.

Piecing Information Together

Problem

How do the skills of observing and inferring help scientists piece together information?

Skills Focus

observing, inferring, predicting

Materials

- paperback book, cut into sections and stapled together
- paper
- pencil

Procedure

1. Examine the small section of the book your teacher gives you. Use your observation skills to list any facts you can state confidently about the book, including its characters, setting, or events.

2. Based on your observations, what can you infer the book is about? Write one or two sentences describing the book's storyline.

3. Get together with a partner and share your book sections, observations, inferences, and story descriptions.

4. Together, write a new one- or two-sentence story description based on your shared observations and information.

5. Get together with another pair of students. Repeat Steps 3 and 4.

6. After you have written your description of the story as a group of four, look back over all your story descriptions. Note how they have changed over time.

Analyze and Conclude

1. Observing Look over the list of observations you made in Step 1. Were any of the observations really inferences? If so, explain why.

2. Inferring How confident did you feel about the inference you made about the storyline in Step 2? How did your confidence level change when your observations included additional sections of the book?

3. Predicting How do you think your level of confidence would change if you observed more and more sections of the book? Explain your reasoning.

4. Communicating Write a paragraph explaining how this activity resembles the work of scientists. How do the observations and inferences you made relate to those that scientists make? What do your story descriptions represent?

More to Explore

Choose a scientific article from a newspaper or magazine. Read the article and identify three observations and three inferences that the scientists made.

FIGURE 23

FIGURE 23
Careers and Science
A knowledge of science is useful in many nonscience careers.

A chef uses knowledge about the chemistry of food and cooking.

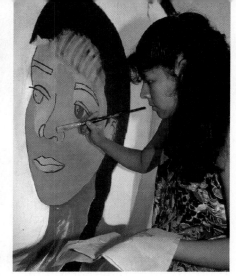
A painter understands the chemistry of paints.

Science in Nonscience Careers

Are scientists the only people who need a knowledge of science on the job? The answer, of course, is no. **In many nonscience careers, a knowledge of science is essential in order to perform the job.** Just a few of the careers that involve science are presented here.

Chef Whether cooking a simple meal or creating a dessert masterpiece, chefs rely on science in the kitchen. Did you know that scrambling an egg involves chemistry or that living organisms are the key to baking delicious breads and cakes? And would you know how to prevent food from spoiling and causing sickness? A lot of science goes into what you eat!

Artist You might be surprised to learn that the work of artists involves science. Sculptors must know about the properties of the materials they use. For example, would bronze be a good material to use for an outdoor sculpture? Glass artists apply the physics of heating and cooling as they shape glass. And painters must understand the properties of the paints, paper, and other materials they work with.

Sound Technician From concert halls to radio stations, sound technicians are busy behind the scenes. Their job is to make sure that the sound quality is at its best. Sound technicians must understand how sound waves travel and how they interact with different materials. Most sound technicians use electronic equipment to adjust the sound quality in different situations.

 **Reading Checkpoint** What is one way that science is involved in an artist's career?

A sound technician uses knowledge about how sound waves travel.

A firefighter must understand the chemistry of fire.

Firefighter When a fire alarm goes off, firefighters do not know what type of fire they will encounter. Is it a grease fire, an electrical fire, or something else? Did you know that some materials actually catch on fire if you spray them with water? Understanding chemistry helps firefighters put out fires and clean up hazardous spills quickly and safely.

 **Reading Checkpoint** **What is one way that science is involved in an artist's career?**

Section 4 Assessment

 **Target Reading Skill** Using Prior Knowledge Review your graphic organizer and revise it based on what you just learned in the section.

Reviewing Key Concepts

1. a. Listing What are the three major branches of science?

  b. Describing Write a one-sentence description of each of the three branches of science.

  c. Classifying Into which branch of science would you classify the following scientists: a scientist studying the organisms in a river; a scientist studying how a river first formed?

2. a. Identifying Give an example of a scientific investigation that involves scientists from different branches working together.

  b. Problem Solving How might an Earth scientist studying volcanoes work together with scientists in each of the other branches of science?

3. a. Reviewing Why should nonscientists study science?

  b. Applying Concepts How would a knowledge of science benefit a gardener?

  c. Making Judgments A friend tells you he doesn't need to study science because he doesn't even know what career he'll want to pursue. What would you tell your friend?

Lab zone At-Home **Activity**

Help Wanted With a family member, look through the job listings in a local newspaper. Cut out four listings—two for science careers and two for nonscience careers. For the science careers, identify the branch of science and the educational background required. For the nonscience careers, identify what science knowledge is needed to perform the job.

1 Thinking Like a Scientist

Key Concepts

- Scientists use skills such as observing, inferring, predicting, classifying, and making models to learn more about the world.
- Successful scientists possess certain important attitudes, or habits of mind, including curiosity, honesty, open-mindedness, skepticism, and creativity.

Key Terms

observing
quantitative observation
qualitative observation
inferring
predicting
classifying
making models
science
skepticism

2 Scientific Inquiry

Key Concepts

- Scientific inquiry refers to the diverse ways in which scientists study the natural world and propose explanations based on the evidence they gather.
- In science, a hypothesis must be testable. This means that researchers must be able to carry out investigations and gather evidence that will either support or disprove the hypothesis.
- Unlike a theory, a scientific law describes an observed pattern in nature without attempting to explain it.

Key Terms

scientific inquiry   operational definition
hypothesis   data
variable   communicating
manipulated variable   scientific theory
responding variable   scientific law
controlled experiment

3 Why Study Science?

Key Concepts

- Being able to understand scientific principles and think scientifically can help you solve problems and answer many questions in your everyday life.
- By having scientific literacy, you will be able to identify good sources of scientific information, evaluate them for accuracy, and apply the knowledge to questions or problems in your life.

Key Term

scientific literacy

4 Careers in Science

Key Concepts

- The three main branches of science are earth and space science, life science, and physical science.
- Although it is convenient to think of science as divided into three branches, these areas are not really separate at all. Most scientific questions being investigated today span the different fields of science.
- In many nonscience careers, a knowledge of science is essential in order to perform the job.

Review and Assessment

Go Online
PHSchool.com
For: Self-Assessment
Visit: PHSchool.com
Web Code: cga-6010

Organizing Information

Identifying Main Ideas Copy the graphic organizer about scientific skills onto a separate sheet of paper. Then complete it and add a title. (For more on Identifying Main Ideas, see the Skills Handbook.)

Main Idea

| Scientists use many different skills to learn more about the world. |

Detail | **Detail** | **Detail** | **Detail** | **Detail**

a. ___?___ | b. ___?___ | c. ___?___ | d. ___?___ | e. ___?___

Reviewing Key Terms

Choose the letter of the best answer.

1. When you explain or interpret an observation, you are
   a. making models.　　b. classifying.
   c. inferring.　　d. predicting.

2. The scientific attitude of having doubt is called
   a. open-mindedness.
   b. curiosity.
   c. honesty.
   d. skepticism.

3. The variable that a scientist intentionally changes in an experiment is called the
   a. manipulated variable.
   b. responding variable.
   c. control.
   d. operational definition.

4. The facts, figures, and other evidence gathered through observations are called
   a. predictions.　　b. hypotheses.
   c. conclusions.　　d. data.

5. Being able to understand basic scientific terms and principles well enough to apply them to your life is called
   a. classifying.
   b. scientific inquiry.
   c. scientific literacy.
   d. controlling variables.

If the statement is true, write *true*. If it is false, change the underlined word or words to make the statement true.

6. Noticing that the sky is dark and hearing thunder in the distance are examples of <u>inferring</u>.

7. When you are <u>predicting</u>, you are making a forecast of what will happen in the future based on your past experiences.

8. A <u>hypothesis</u> is a factor that can change in an experiment.

9. A <u>scientific theory</u> is a well-tested explanation for a wide range of observations.

10. <u>Life science</u> includes the study of motion, sound, light, electricity, and magnetism.

Writing in Science

Description Think about the ways in which the police who investigate crimes act like scientists. In a paragraph, describe the scientific skills that police use in their work.

Discovery CHANNEL SCHOOL

What Is Science?
Video Preview
Video Field Trip
► Video Assessment

Review and Assessment

Checking Concepts

11. What is the difference between inferring and predicting?

12. In your own words, explain briefly what science is.

13. Why is it important to report experimental results honestly even when the results go against your hypothesis?

14. What are some ways scientists communicate with one another?

15. Give an example from your life in which having scientific literacy was important.

16. How do the different branches of science depend on one another?

Thinking Critically

17. Inferring Suppose you come home to the scene below. What can you infer happened while you were gone?

18. Problem Solving Suppose you would like to find out which dog food your dog likes best. What variables would you need to control in your experiment?

19. Making Judgments You read an ad claiming that scientific studies prove that frozen fruit is more nutritious than canned vegetables. What questions would you want answered before you accept this claim?

20. Making Generalizations Your friend tells you that she wants to become an astronaut and therefore only needs to study space science. Do you agree with this statement? Why or why not?

Applying Skills

Use the data table below to answer Questions 21–25.

Three students conducted a controlled experiment to find out how walking and running affected their heart rates.

Effect of Activity on Heart Rate (in beats per minute)

Student	Heart Rate (at rest)	Heart Rate (walking)	Heart Rate (running)
1	70	90	115
2	72	80	100
3	80	100	120

21. Controlling Variables What is the manipulated variable in this experiment? What is the responding variable?

22. Developing Hypotheses What hypothesis might this experiment be testing?

23. Predicting Based on this experiment and what you know about exercising, predict how the students' heart rates would change while they are resting after a long run.

24. Designing Experiments Design a controlled experiment to determine which activity has more of an effect on a person's heart rate—jumping rope or doing push-ups.

25. Drawing Conclusions What does the data indicate about the increased physical activity and heart rate?

Lab zone Chapter Project

Performance Assessment Create a poster that summarizes your experiment for the class. Your poster should include the question you tested, how you tested it, the data you collected, and what conclusion you drew from your experiment. What problems did you encounter while carrying out your experiment? Is additional testing necessary?

Standardized Test Prep

Choose the letter of the best answer.

1. What would be the best way to determine which brand of paper towels is the "strongest when wet"?

  A comparing television commercials that demonstrate the strength of paper towels

  B tearing different brands of towels when they are wet to feel which seems strongest

  C comparing how much weight each brand of towel can hold when wet before it breaks

  D conducting a survey of consumers, professional cooks, and restaurant staff

2. Which of the following habits of mind do good scientists possess?

  F curiosity about the natural world

  G open-mindedness about their findings and those of other scientists

  H honesty in reporting observations and results

  J all of the above

The graph below compares how well two different brands of insulated mugs retained heat. Use the graph and your knowledge of science to answer Questions 3–4.

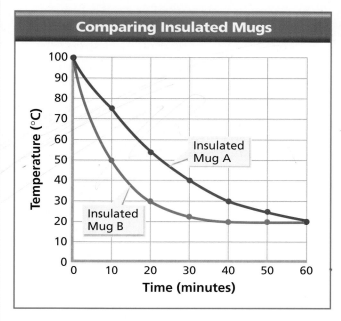

3. What was the manipulated variable in this experiment?

  A the temperature of the water

  B location of the travel mug

  C brand of travel mug

  D the length of time the water was allowed to cool

4. What conclusion can you draw from this experiment?

  F There is no difference between brands A and B.

  G Brand A keeps water warmer longer than brand B.

  H Brand B keeps water warmer longer than brand A.

  J Brand B seems to add heat to the water.

Constructed Response

5. Advertisements for three brands of plant food each claim that their brand makes plants grow fastest. How would you design an experiment to test which brand works best?

Chapter 2

The Work of Scientists

Chapter Preview

interactive Textbook

This scientist studies young bearded seals that live in subzero waters near Norway. ▶

Discovery
CHANNEL
SCHOOL

The Work of Scientists
▶ **Video Preview**
Video Field Trip
Video Assessment

Lab zone™ Chapter **Project**

Design and Build a Scale Model

How do scientists study something as large as the solar system or as tiny as an atom? One tool they use is a model. Models help scientists picture things that are difficult to see or understand. In this chapter project, you will create a three-dimensional model of a building or room.

Your Goal To create a three-dimensional model that shows the size relationships among the different parts of the model

To complete this project, you must

● measure or find the actual dimensions of the structure to be modeled
● sketch your model on graph paper and calculate the size of each part you will include
● construct your three-dimensional model
● follow the safety guidelines in Appendix A

Plan It! Choose a room in your house or school, or a familiar building to model. Think about how you could construct a smaller replica of that room or building. Preview the chapter to find out how scientists make measurements. Then write a brief plan detailing how you will proceed with this project. Make sure your plan includes a sketch and a list of the materials you will use. After your teacher approves your plan, start working on your model.

Measurement—A Common Language

Reading Preview

Key Concepts
- Why do scientists use a standard measurement system?
- What are the SI units of measure for length, mass, volume, density, time, and temperature?
- How are conversion factors useful?

Key Terms
- metric system • SI • mass
- weight • volume • meniscus
- density

Target Reading Skill
Comparing and Contrasting
As you read, compare and contrast different types of measurement by completing a table like the one below.

Measurement

Characteristic	Length	Mass
Definition		
SI unit		
Measuring tool		

Lab zone **Discover Activity**

How Many Shoes?

1. Trace an outline of your shoe onto a piece of paper. Cut out your pattern.
2. Use your pattern to measure the length of your classroom in "shoes."
3. Compare your measurement to those of three classmates. Did you all measure the same number of "shoes"?

Think It Over
Inferring Why do you think it is important that people use standard units of measurement?

Did you ever ask a relative for an old family recipe? If so, the answer might have been, "Use just the right amount of flour and water. Add a spoonful of oil and a pinch of salt. Bake it for awhile until it looks just right."

Instructions like these would be difficult to follow. How much flour is "just the right amount"? How big is a spoonful or a pinch? It would be impossible for you to know what your relative had in mind. You could end up with disastrous results.

◄ In tasks such as cooking, measurements can be critical!

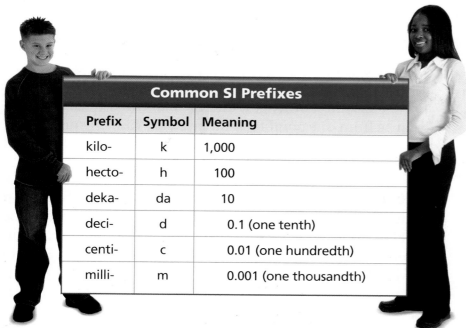

Common SI Prefixes		
Prefix	Symbol	Meaning
kilo-	k	1,000
hecto-	h	100
deka-	da	10
deci-	d	0.1 (one tenth)
centi-	c	0.01 (one hundredth)
milli-	m	0.001 (one thousandth)

FIGURE 1
SI units, based on multiples of 10, are easy to use. Knowing what the prefixes mean can help you judge how big or small a measurement is.
Calculating *How much larger is a* kilo- *than a* deka-?

A Standard Measurement System

The recipe example illustrates the importance of using a standard system of measurement. This is especially true in science. Using the same system of measurement minimizes confusion among scientists all over the world.

The Metric System More than 200 years ago, most countries used their own measurement systems. Sometimes two or more different systems were used in the same country. In the 1790s, scientists in France developed a universal system of measurement called the metric system. The **metric system** is a system of measurement based on the number 10.

The International System of Units (SI) Modern scientists use a version of the metric system called the International System of Units, abbreviated as **SI** (for the French, *Système International d'Unités*). Scientists all over the world use SI units to measure length, volume, mass, density, temperature, and time. **Using SI as the standard system of measurement allows scientists to compare data and communicate with each other about their results.** In this book and others in the *Science Explorer* program, you will use both SI and other metric units.

Figure 1 lists the prefixes used to name the most common SI units. Because they are based on multiples of 10, SI units are easy to use. Each unit is ten times larger than the next smallest unit and one tenth the size of the next largest unit. This is similar to our money system, in which a dime is worth ten times more than a penny, but one tenth as much as a dollar.

Reading Checkpoint SI units are based on multiples of what number?

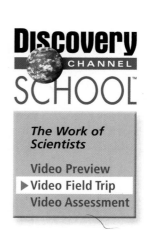

DISCOVERY
CHANNEL
SCHOOL

The Work of Scientists

Video Preview
▶ Video Field Trip
Video Assessment

Common Conversions for Length	
1 km	= 1,000 m
1 m	= 100 cm
1 m	= 1,000 mm
1 cm	= 10 mm

Length

How far can you throw a softball? Can you judge by eye how far the ball travels? A better way to find out would be to measure the distance, or length, that the ball travels. Length is the distance from one point to another. In the case of your softball throw, it would be from the point where you release the ball to the point where it first hits the ground.

Units of Length The basic unit of length in the SI system is the meter (m). One meter is about the distance from the floor to a doorknob. A softball throw would be measured in meters. So would your height. Most students your age are between 1.5 and 2 meters tall.

Science and History

Measurement Systems

Like so much else in science, systems of measurement developed gradually over time in different parts of the world.

640 B.C. Standard Units of Weight

Merchants in the Middle East and Mediterranean used units of weight to be sure that they received the correct amount of gold and silver in trade and to check the purity of the metal. A *talent* was about 25 kilograms, and a *mina* was about 500 grams. The Lydians minted the first true coins to have standard weight and value.

200 B.C. Standard Measures

Shih Huang Ti, the first emperor of China, set standards for weight, length, and volume. He also improved travel conditions by setting standards for the widths of roads and for the distance between chariot wheels.

1400 B.C. A Simple Balance

The ancient Egyptians developed the first known weighing instrument, a simple balance with a pointer. Earlier, they had been the first to standardize a measure of length. The length, called a cubit, was originally defined as the distance between the elbow and the tip of the middle finger.

| 1500 B.C. | 1000 B.C. | 500 B.C. | A.D. 1 |

To measure objects smaller than a meter, scientists use units called the centimeter (cm) or the millimeter (mm). The prefix *centi-* means "one-hundredth," while the prefix *milli-* means one-thousandth. One meter, then, is equal to 100 centimeters or 1,000 millimeters. The length of a typical sheet of loose-leaf paper is 28 centimeters, which is equal to 280 millimeters.

What unit would you use to measure a long distance, such as the distance between two cities? For such measurements, scientists use a unit known as the kilometer (km). The prefix *kilo-* means one thousand. There are 1,000 meters in a kilometer. If you were to draw a straight line between San Francisco and Boston, the line would measure about 4,300 kilometers.

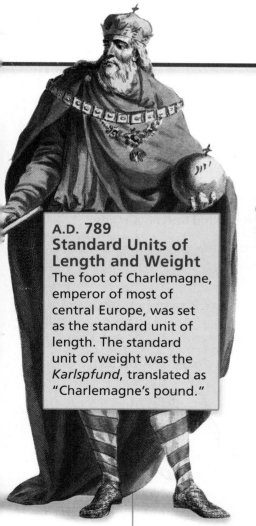

A.D. 789
Standard Units of Length and Weight
The foot of Charlemagne, emperor of most of central Europe, was set as the standard unit of length. The standard unit of weight was the *Karlspfund*, translated as "Charlemagne's pound."

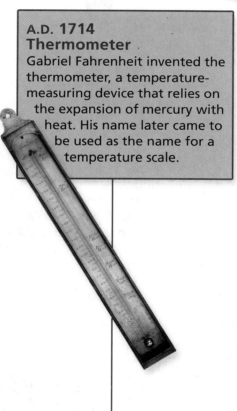

A.D. 1714
Thermometer
Gabriel Fahrenheit invented the thermometer, a temperature-measuring device that relies on the expansion of mercury with heat. His name later came to be used as the name for a temperature scale.

A.D. 1983
International Standards
The International Bureau of Weights and Measures in France defined a single set of standard units. Scientists throughout the world use these units in their work. The official kilogram measure, shown above, is kept in a vacuum chamber.

| A.D. 500 | A.D. 1000 | A.D. 1500 | A.D. 2000 |

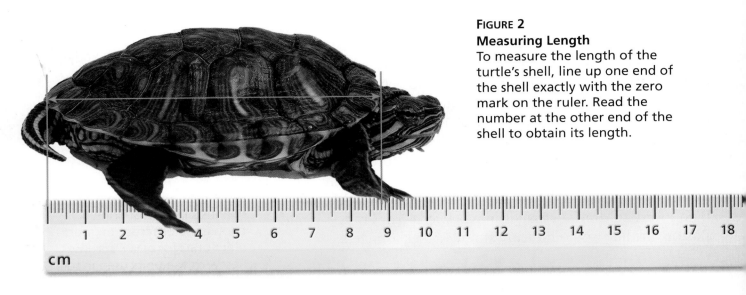

Measuring Length A very common tool used to measure length is the metric ruler. As you can see in Figure 2, a metric ruler is divided into centimeters. The centimeter markings are the longer lines numbered 1, 2, 3, and so on. Each centimeter is then divided into 10 millimeters, which are marked by the shorter lines.

To use a metric ruler, line one end of the object up exactly with the zero mark. Then read the number at the other end of the object. The shell of the turtle in Figure 2 is 8.8 centimeters, or 88 millimeters, long.

 **Reading Checkpoint** One centimeter is divided into how many millimeters?

Mass

Can you lift a bicycle with one finger? Probably not, unless the bicycle's frame is made of titanium, a strong but very light metal. Most bike racers use titanium frames because the bike's low mass allows them to ride faster. **Mass** is a measure of the amount of matter an object contains.

Units of Mass **The basic unit of mass in the SI system is the kilogram (kg).** The kilogram is a useful unit when measuring the mass of objects such as bicycles, cars, or people. The mass of a wooden baseball bat is about 1 kilogram.

To measure the mass of smaller objects, you will use a unit known as the gram (g). As you can guess, there are 1,000 grams in a kilogram. A large paper clip has a mass of about 1 gram. Even smaller masses are measured in milligrams (mg). There are 1,000 milligrams in one gram.

Common Conversions for Mass	
1 kg	= 1,000 g
1 g	= 1,000 mg

Measuring Mass To find the mass of an object, you may use a balance like the one in Figure 3. This balance, known as a triple-beam balance, works by comparing the mass of the object you are measuring to a known mass. When you use a triple-beam balance, you first place the object on the pan. You then shift the riders on the beams until they balance the mass of the object. You can find step-by-step instructions for using a triple-beam balance in Appendix C.

The Difference Between Mass and Weight Mass is often confused with weight. But weight is not the same thing as mass. **Weight** is a measure of the force of gravity acting on an object. As you probably know, you can measure an object's weight using a scale. When you stand on a scale, gravity pulls you downward, compressing springs inside the scale. The more you weigh, the more the springs compress, and the higher the reading.

If, however, you were to weigh yourself on the moon, you would obtain a very different reading. Because the force of gravity is much weaker on the moon than on Earth, the springs inside the scale would compress much less. You would weigh less on the moon. But how would your mass compare? Because mass measures the amount of matter an object contains, it remains constant wherever an object may be. Your mass on the moon is the same as your mass on Earth. You can see why scientists prefer to use mass, rather than weight, when making measurements.

 **What is weight?**

Lab zone Skills **Activity**

Measuring

Use a balance to determine the mass of the following objects

- a CD
- a crumpled sheet of notebook paper
- this textbook

Compare your measurements to those of a classmate. How close are the two sets of measurements?

FIGURE 3
Measuring Mass
You can use a triple-beam balance to find the mass of small objects. To measure mass, place the object on the pan and shift the riders on each beam until the pointer stops at zero. **Observing** *What is the mass of this turtle?*

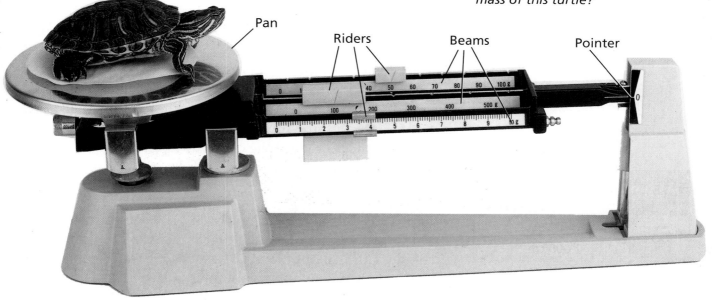

Pan   Riders   Beams   Pointer

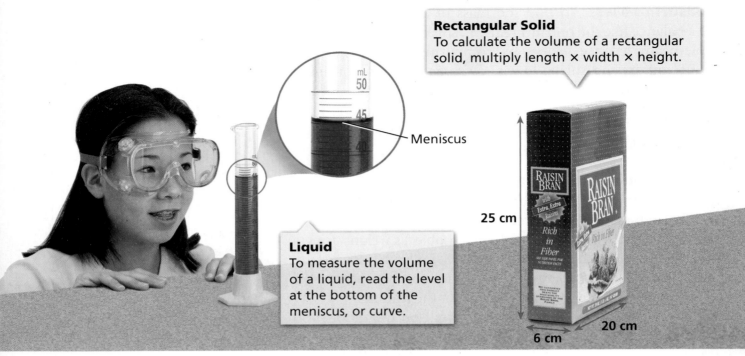

Rectangular Solid
To calculate the volume of a rectangular solid, multiply length × width × height.

Meniscus

Liquid
To measure the volume of a liquid, read the level at the bottom of the meniscus, or curve.

25 cm

6 cm

20 cm

FIGURE 4

Measuring Volume

Volume is the amount of space an object takes up. Measuring the volume of liquids, rectangular solids, and irregular solids requires different methods.

Observing *What is the proper way to read a meniscus?*

Common Conversions for Volume	
1 L	= 1,000 mL
1 L	= 1,000 cm³
1 mL	= 1 cm³

Volume

Do you drink milk or orange juice with breakfast? If so, how much do you have? You probably don't measure it out; you just pour it into a glass. You decide when to stop pouring by observing the amount of space it fills in the glass. **Volume** is the amount of space an object takes up.

Volume of Liquids To measure the volume of a liquid, scientists use a unit known as the liter (L). You have probably seen 1-liter and 2-liter bottles of beverages at the grocery store. You can measure smaller liquid volumes using milliliters (mL). There are 1,000 milliliters in a liter.

To measure the volume of a liquid, just pour it into a container with markings that show the volume. Scientists commonly use a graduated cylinder to measure liquid volumes. The graduated cylinder in Figure 4 is marked off in 1-milliliter segments. Notice that the top surface of the water in the graduated cylinder is curved. This curve is called the **meniscus.** To determine the volume of water, you should read the milliliter marking at the bottom of the curve.

Volume of Rectangular Solids How can you determine the volume of a solid object, such as a cereal box? The unit you would use is the cubic centimeter (cm^3). A cubic centimeter is equal to the volume of a cube that measures 1 centimeter on each side. This is about the size of a sugar cube. One cubic centimeter is exactly equal to one milliliter.

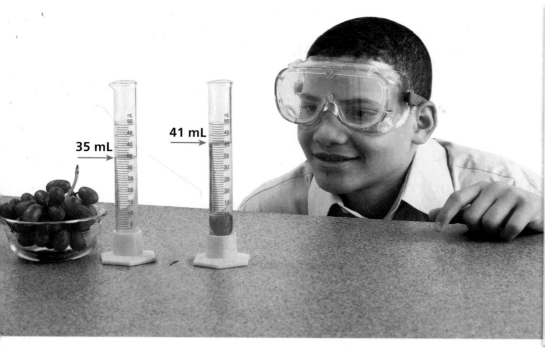

Irregular Solids
To measure the volume of an irregular solid, use the water displacement method.

1 Record the volume of water in the grad-uated cylinder.

2 Carefully place the irregular solid into the water. Record the volume of the water plus the object.

3 Subtract the volume of the water alone from the volume of the water plus the object.

35 mL

41 mL

For solids with larger volumes, scientists use the SI unit known as the cubic meter (m^3). A cubic meter is equal to the volume of a cube that measures 1 meter on each side.

You can calculate the volume of a regular solid using this formula:

Volume = Length × Width × Height

Suppose that a cereal box is 20 centimeters long, 6 centimeters wide, and 25 centimeters high. The volume of the box is

Volume = 20 cm × 6 cm × 25 cm = 3,000 cm^3

Notice that, when you calculate volume, in addition to multiplying the numbers (20 × 6 × 25 = 3,000), you also multiply the units (cm × cm × cm = cm^3). Therefore, you must be sure to use the same units for all measurements when calculating the volume of a regular solid.

Volume of Irregular Solids Suppose you wanted to mea-sure the volume of a rock. Because of its irregular shape, you can't measure a rock's length, width, or height. How, then, could you find its volume? One method is to immerse the object in water, and measure how much the water level rises. This method is shown in Figure 4.

 **Reading Checkpoint** What is a cubic meter?

Go Online
PHSchool.com

For: More on measurement
Visit: PHSchool.com
Web Code: cgd-6021

Density

As you can see in Figure 5, two objects of the same size can have very different masses. This is because different materials have different densities. **Density** is a measure of how much mass is contained in a given volume. To calculate the density of an object, divide its mass by its volume.

$$\text{Density} = \frac{\text{Mass}}{\text{Volume}}$$

Units of Density Because density is actually made up of two other measurements—mass and volume—an object's density is expressed as a combination of two units. Two common units of density are grams per cubic centimeter (g/cm^3) and grams per milliliter (g/mL). In each case, the numerator is a measure of mass while the denominator is a measure of volume.

FIGURE 5
Comparing Densities
Although the bowling ball and beach ball have the same volume, one contains much more mass than the other. *Inferring Which item has the greater density?*

Math Practice

1. What is the density of a wood block with a volume of 125 cm^3 and a mass of 57 g?

2. What is the density of a liquid with a mass of 45 g and a volume of 48 mL?

Math Sample Problem

Calculating Density

Suppose that a metal object has a mass of 57 g and a volume of 21 cm^3. Calculate its density.

1 Read and Understand
What information are you given?
   Mass of metal object = 57 g
   Volume of metal object = 21 cm^3

2 Plan and Solve
What quantity are you trying to calculate?
   The density of the metal object = ■

What formula contains the given quantities and the unknown quantity?

   $$\text{Density} = \frac{\text{Mass}}{\text{Volume}}$$

Perform the calculation.

   $$\text{Density} = \frac{\text{Mass}}{\text{Volume}} = \frac{57\text{ g}}{21\text{ cm}^3} = 2.7\text{ g/cm}^3$$

3 Look Back and Check
Does your answer make sense?
   The answer tells you that the metal object has a density of 2.7 g/cm^3. The answer makes sense because it is the same as the density of a known metal—aluminum.

Densities of Common Substances The table in Figure 6 lists the densities of some common substances. The density of a substance is the same for all samples of that substance. For example, all samples of pure gold—no matter how large or small—have a density of 19.3 g/cm³.

Once you know an object's density, you can determine whether or not the object will float in a given liquid. An object will float if it is less dense than the surrounding liquid. For example, the density of water is 1 g/cm³. A piece of wood with a density of 0.8 g/cm³ will float in water. A ring made of pure silver, which has a density of 10.5 g/cm³, will sink.

 **Will an object with a density of 0.7 g/cm³ float or sink in water?**

Time

The crowd cheers wildly as you near the finish line. You push your legs to run even faster in the final moments of the race. From the corner of your eye, you see your opponent catching up to you. At moments like this, just one second can mean the difference between winning and losing.

Units of Time **The second (s) is the SI unit used to measure time.** Your heart beats about once per second—when you are not running, that is! The second can easily be divided by multiples of 10, like the other SI units. For example, a millisecond (ms) is one-thousandth of a second. Longer periods of time are expressed in minutes or hours. There are 60 seconds in a minute, and 60 minutes in an hour.

Measuring Time Clocks and watches are used to measure time. Some clocks are more accurate than others. Some digital stopwatches, which are used to time races, can measure time accurately to one hundredth of a second.

 **How many milliseconds are in one second?**

Densities of Some Common Substances	
Substance	**Density (g/cm³)**
Air	0.001
Ice	0.9
Water	1.0
Aluminum	2.7
Gold	19.3

FIGURE 6
The density of a substance stays the same no matter how large or small a sample of the substance is. Applying Concepts *How could you use density to determine whether a bar of metal is pure gold?*

FIGURE 7
Measuring Time
A stopwatch can be used to measure time.

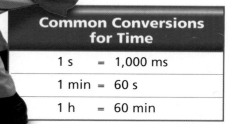

Common Conversions for Time		
1 s	=	1,000 ms
1 min	=	60 s
1 h	=	60 min

Temperature

As you head out the door each morning, one of the first things you might notice is the temperature. Is it cold out this morning? How high will the temperature rise?

Units of Temperature Scientists commonly use the Celsius temperature scale. On the Celsius scale, water freezes at 0°C and boils at 100°C. There are exactly 100 degrees between the freezing point and boiling point of water. Normal human body temperature is about 37°C.

In addition to the Celsius scale, scientists sometimes use another temperature scale, called the Kelvin scale. In fact, the kelvin (K) is the official SI unit for temperature. Units on the Kelvin scale are the same size as those on the Celsius scale. Figure 8 compares these two temperature scales.

Zero on the Kelvin scale (0 K) is the temperature that scientists consider to be the coldest possible temperature. Nothing can get colder than this temperature, called absolute zero. Absolute zero is equal to –273°C on the Celsius scale. The Kelvin scale is useful because it does not have negative numbers to complicate calculations.

Measuring Temperature You can measure temperature using a thermometer. When you first place the thermometer in a substance, the liquid inside the thermometer will begin to move up or down. Wait until the level of the liquid stops changing. Then read the number next to the top of the liquid in the thermometer.

 **Reading Checkpoint** What is the official SI unit for temperature?

Converting Between Units

Do you have a jar where you keep all your pennies? Suppose you counted your penny collection and discovered that you had 236 pennies. How many dollars does that equal? With only a little thought, you could probably answer, "$2.36."

Just like converting between dollars and cents, it is often necessary to convert from one unit of measurement to another. **To convert one measurement to another, you need to know the appropriate conversion factor. A conversion factor is an equation that shows how two units of measurement are related.** For conversion factors, refer to the conversion tables included throughout this section.

Figure 8 — Temperature diagram

	Celsius (°C)	Kelvin (K)
Boiling Point of Water	100	373
Freezing Point of Water	0	273
Absolute Zero	–273	0

FIGURE 8
Measuring Temperature
Scientists use the Celsius and Kelvin scales to measure temperature. Units on both scales are the same size.
Observing At what temperature on the Kelvin scale does water boil?

Common Conversions for Temperature	
0°C =	273 K
100°C =	373 K

Suppose you walk 1.5 kilometers to a friend's house. How many meters have you walked? To convert 1.5 kilometers to meters, follow these steps:

1 Begin by writing down the measurement you want to convert.

2 Find a conversion factor that relates the two units you are converting.

3 Write the conversion factor as a fraction. Make sure to place the units you are converting from in the denominator.

4 Multiply the measurement you are converting from by the fraction. When you do this, the units in the measurement will cancel out with the units in the denominator of the fraction. Your answer will then be in the units you are converting to.

By converting between units, you now know that you walked 1,500 meters to your friend's house.

 Reading Checkpoint **What is a conversion factor?**

1 1.5 km = _?_ m

2 1 km = 1,000 m

3 $\dfrac{1{,}000 \text{ m}}{1 \text{ km}}$

4 1.5 km × $\dfrac{1{,}000 \text{ m}}{1 \text{ km}}$ = 1,500 m

1.5 km = 1,500 m

FIGURE 9
Converting Between Units
Using the appropriate conversion factor, you can easily convert one unit of measurement to another. This example shows how to convert 1.5 kilometers to meters.

Section 1 Assessment

Target Reading Skill

Comparing and Contrasting Use the information in your table about the different types of measurement to answer Question 2.

Reviewing Key Concepts

1. a. **Identifying** What is the standard measurement system used by scientists around the world?
   b. **Predicting** Suppose that two scientists use different measurement systems in their work. What problems might arise if they shared their data?

2. a. **Listing** What SI unit would you use to measure the length of a baseball bat? What SI unit would you use to measure the mass of a baseball?
   b. **Estimating** Estimate the length of a baseball bat and mass of a baseball. Be sure to use the appropriate SI units in your predictions. How could you determine how close your estimates are?

   c. **Problem Solving** Outline a step-by-step method for determining the density of a baseball.

3. a. **Reviewing** What is a conversion factor?
   b. **Identifying** What conversion factor would you use to convert between liters and milliliters?
   c. **Calculating** Your cat's bowl holds 0.25 liters of liquid. How many milliliters of water can you pour into the bowl?

Math Practice

Two solid cubes have the same mass. They each have a mass of 50 g.

4. **Calculating Density** Cube A has a volume of 2 cm × 2 cm × 2 cm. What is its density?

5. **Calculating Density** Cube B has a volume of 4 cm × 4 cm × 4 cm. What is its density?

Backpack Basics

Problem

Which backpack is a better choice for carrying the recommended safe load of books?

Skills Focus

measuring, calculating, drawing conclusions

Materials

- balance   • 5–6 textbooks   • meter stick
- 2 backpacks (one large and one small)

Procedure

PART 1 Determining Your Maximum Safe Load

1. To prevent back problems, experts recommend that the mass of the backpack you carry should be no greater than 15 percent of your body mass. Use the table below to find your "maximum safe load."

Determining Maximum Safe Load	
Body Mass kg (lbs)	Maximum Safe Load (kg)
30 (66)	4.5
35 (77)	5.3
40 (88)	6.0
45 (99)	6.8
50 (110)	7.5
55 (121)	8.3
60 (132)	9.0
65 (143)	9.8
70 (154)	10.5
75 (165)	11.3
80 (176)	12.0
85 (187)	12.8

2. To determine how many textbooks equal your maximum safe load, use a balance to find the mass of one textbook. Next, divide your maximum safe load by the mass of the textbook. Your answer is the number of textbooks (of that size) you can safely carry in a backpack.

PART 2 Comparing Backpacks

3. Your teacher will give you two backpacks—one large and one small. Load each backpack with the number of textbooks you calculated in Step 2. Carry each backpack on your back for one minute and note how it feels. Also, observe how empty or full each backpack is.

4. Using a meter stick, measure the length, width, and height in centimeters of each backpack. Your partner should stretch out the backpacks fully as you measure them. Record the dimensions in a data table like the one at the top of the next page.

5. Calculate the volume of each backpack using this formula:

    Volume = Length × Width × Height

    Record the volumes in your data table.

6. Calculate the approximate volume of the textbook you used in Part 1. Measure its length, width, and height in centimeters, and then multiply these measurements together.

Data Table						
Backpack	Length (cm)	Width (cm)	Height (cm)	Volume (cm³)	Total Number of Textbooks	Total Mass of Textbooks (kg)
1						
2						

7. Calculate the total number of textbooks that could fit into each backpack by dividing the volume of each backpack (from Step 5) by the volume of one textbook (from Step 6). Record the results for each backpack in your data table.

8. Calculate the total mass of textbooks that could fit into each backpack by multiplying the mass of one textbook (from Step 2) by the total number of textbooks that fit into each (from Step 7). Record the results in your data table.

Analyze and Conclude

1. **Observing** Is each backpack large enough to carry your maximum safe load? What differences did you notice between the two backpacks when carrying this load of books?

2. **Measuring** How do the two backpacks compare in volume? What is the total mass of books that each backpack could carry?

3. **Calculating** Calculate how many times your maximum safe load each backpack could carry. (*Hint:* Divide the total mass of books from Step 8 by your maximum safe load in Step 1.)

4. **Drawing Conclusions** Based on the calculations and observations you made in this lab, what are some of the pros and cons of each backpack?

5. **Communicating** Choose one of the backpacks and write an advertisement for it. In your advertisement, be sure to explain why it would be the best choice for students.

More to Explore

For a week, record the actual mass of the backpack you carry to school each day. Then calculate the average (mean) mass of your backpack. How does this compare to your recommended maximum safe load?

Should the United States Go Metric?

On a long car ride, have you ever asked, "Are we there yet?" If the driver answered, "We're 30 kilometers away," would you know whether you were close to your destination or far away?

As a U.S. resident, you probably have no trouble understanding English units, which include miles, feet, pounds, and gallons. Metric units, however, may be more unfamiliar. But most countries in the world use the metric system. Should the United States convert to metric or continue using the English system?

The Issues

Why Change?

People in the United States are comfortable with the English system of measurement. If the country converted to metric, citizens might have a hard time buying products or calculating distances. These problems may not disappear overnight.

Businesses in the United States rely on the English system. Many of the tools and machines that manufacture goods are based on the English system, as are the goods themselves. To go metric, the machines would have to be replaced and the goods repackaged. This could cost millions of dollars.

Why Be Left Behind?

Supporters of the metric system point out how easy it is to learn. Because metric units are based on the number 10, converting from kilometers to meters, for example, is simple. In contrast, converting miles to feet, or gallons to ounces, is more complicated. Schoolchildren could master the metric system much more quickly than the English system.

Furthermore, conversion may help the United States stay competitive in foreign trade. Many U.S. businesses sell their products in other countries. But people worldwide prefer products labeled in units they know—in this case, metric units. They may avoid products that are not made to metric standards. In fact, by 2010, products sold in Europe must be labeled in metric units only.

Why Not Compromise?

The next time you drink a bottle of juice, look at its label. Most likely, it includes both English and metric units. Labels like these are a compromise. They allow users of both measurement systems to know exactly what they are buying.

Some people feel that such a compromise works well enough. People who need to use the metric system, such as those in science and industry, should be able to use it. However, those who prefer to use English units should be able to do so as well.

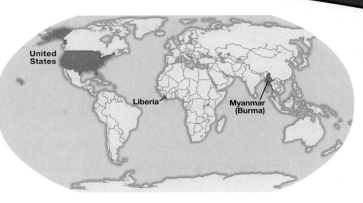

The countries in red currently use the English system of measurement.

You Decide

1. Identify the Problem
In your own words, state the advantages and disadvantages of converting to the metric system.

2. Analyze the Options
Do some research on countries that have recently gone metric. What problems did these countries face? How did they overcome the problems? Did the benefits of converting to the metric system outweigh the costs?

3. Find a Solution
Take a stance on this issue. Then engage in a class debate about whether or not the United States should convert to the metric system. Support your opinion with facts from this feature and from your research.

For: More on going metric
Visit: PHSchool.com
Web Code: cgh-6020

Mathematics and Science

Reading Preview

Key Concepts
- What math skills do scientists use in collecting data and making measurements?
- What math skills help scientists analyze their data?

Key Terms
- estimate • accuracy
- precision • significant figures
- percent error • mean
- median • mode

Target Reading Skill

Asking Questions Before you read, preview the red headings. In a graphic organizer like the one below, ask a *what, how,* or *why* question for each heading. As you read, write the answers to your questions.

Mathematics and Science

Question	Answer
What does estimation have to do with science?	Scientists use estimation . . .

Discover **Activity**
Lab zone

How Many Marbles Are There?

1. Your teacher will give you a jar full of marbles.
2. With a partner, come up with a way to determine the number of marbles in the jar without actually counting them.
3. Use your method to determine the number of marbles. Write down your answer.
4. Compare the method you used to that of another group.

Think It Over
Predicting Which method do you think led to a more accurate answer? Why?

Here's a riddle for you. What do the following things have in common: microscopes, telescopes, thermometers, balances, and mathematics? Do you give up? The answer is that they are all tools that scientists use.

Does it surprise you that mathematics is included in this list? You probably think of mathematics as something that is separate from science. But it is not. In fact, mathematics is sometimes called the "language of science."

Mathematics is essential for asking and answering questions about the natural world. From making measurements to collecting and analyzing data, scientists use math every day. This section focuses on some important math skills you will use in science class.

Estimation

Have you ever been on stage and wondered how many people there were in the audience? Maybe you counted the number of people in one row and multiplied by the number of rows. This would be one way to arrive at an estimate. An **estimate** is an approximation of a number based on reasonable assumptions. Estimating is not the same as guessing because an estimate is based on known information.

FIGURE 10
Estimation
Estimation is an important math skill that scientists use in their work. Estimating is a quick way to determine the large number of birds in this photo.

There are 36 birds in the highlighted area. The total area is six times larger. Thus, you can estimate that there are 36 × 6, or 216 birds in total.

Scientists must sometimes rely on estimates when they cannot obtain exact numbers. Astronomers, for example, can't actually measure the distance between stars. Park rangers can't count the number of trees in large forests. Instead, scientists find ways to make reasonable estimates. An astronomer's estimate might be based on indirect measurements, calculations, and models. A park ranger's estimate might be based on a sample. The ranger could count the trees in a small area and then multiply to estimate the number in the entire forest.

 **Reading Checkpoint** What are estimates based on?

Math Skills

Area
The area of a surface is the amount of space it covers. To find the area, multiply its length by its width. Remember to multiply the units as well.

Area = Length × Width

Suppose the area highlighted in Figure 10 measures 12.0 m by 11.0 m.

$$\text{Area} = 12.0 \text{ m} \times 11.0 \text{ m}$$
$$= 132 \text{ m}^2$$

Practice Problems Calculate the area of the following.

1. A room 4.0 m long and 3.0 m wide
2. A ticket stub 5.1 mm long and 2.62 mm wide

▲ Neither Precise nor Accurate

▲ Precise but Not Accurate

Accuracy and Precision

Suppose you were to meet a friend at 4:00 P.M. Your friend arrives at 4:15 and says, "But it's 4:00 according to all the clocks in my house." The problem is that your friend's clocks do not show the accurate, or correct, time. **Accuracy** refers to how close a measurement is to the true or accepted value. An accurate clock would read 4:00 P.M. However, if all of your friend's clocks are always 15 minutes late, they can be said to be precise. **Precision** refers to how close a group of measurements are to each other.

Accuracy Versus Precision As you can see from the clock example, accuracy and precision do not mean the same thing. To understand the difference, think about a game of darts. As Figure 11 shows, accurate throws land close to the bull's-eye. Precise throws, on the other hand, land close to one another.

Accuracy and Precision in Measurements **Both accuracy and precision are important when you make measurements.** For example, suppose your younger sister wants to find out how tall she has grown. When you measure her height, the measurement needs to be accurate, or close to her true height. The measurement also needs to be precise. This means that if you measured her height several times, you would get the same measurement again and again.

How can you be sure that a measurement you make is both accurate and precise? First, you need to use a high-quality measurement tool. Next, you need to make your measurement carefully. Finally, you need to repeat the measurement a few times. If you follow these steps and get the same measurement each time, then you can feel confident that your measurement is reliable.

 Reading Checkpoint **What does an accurate measurement mean?**

FIGURE 11
Accuracy and Precision
In a game of darts, it's easy to see the difference between accurate throws and precise throws. In order to hit the bull's-eye consistently, you need both accuracy and precision!

▲ Both Precise and Accurate

I am certain of the "5" but am estimating the "3." Therefore, my measurement can only be expressed to two significant figures, 5.3 cm.

Significant Figures

Whenever you measure something, you give meaning, or significance, to each digit in the measurement. In fact, scientists use the term **significant figures** to refer to the digits in a measurement. **The significant figures in a measurement include all of the digits that have been measured exactly, plus one digit whose value has been estimated.**

For example, you might estimate that the tile in Figure 12 is 5.3 centimeters long—you are certain of the 5, but you have estimated the 3 on the end. To find the number of significant figures in a measurement, count the number of digits that were accurately measured, plus the one estimated digit. Therefore, a measurement of 5.3 centimeters has two significant figures.

Adding or Subtracting Measurements When you add or subtract measurements, the answer can only have as many figures after the decimal point as the measurement with the fewest figures after the decimal. For example, suppose you add a tile that is 5.3 centimeters long to a row of tiles that is 21.94 centimeters long.

> 5.3   cm (1 significant figure after decimal)
> + 21.94 cm (2 significant figures after decimal)
> 27.24 cm = 27.2 cm (1 significant figure after decimal)

The answer, "27.2 centimeters," has only one significant figure after the decimal point because the measurement 5.3 centimeters has only one figure after the decimal point.

Why is it incorrect to express your answer as 27.24 centimeters? The reason is that your answer would appear to be more accurate than it really is. Remember that when you first measured the tile, you estimated the "3" in the tenths place. When you add that number to another, the number in the tenths place in the sum is still only an estimate. If you expressed your answer as "27.24" centimeters, the "2" in the tenths place would appear to be an exact measurement, rather than an estimate.

FIGURE 12
Significant Figures
A measurement should contain only those numbers that are significant—all of the digits that have been measured exactly plus one you have estimated.
Measuring *Why can you only report the length of the tile to two significant figures?*

Go Online
SCiLINKS NSTA

For: Links on math and science
Visit: www.SciLinks.org
Web Code: scn-1622

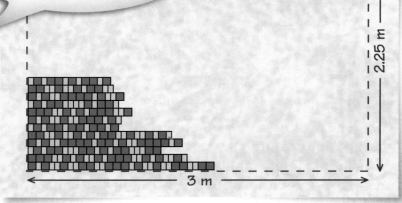

The length "2.25 m" has three significant figures, while the width "3 m" has one. Therefore, my answer can only have one significant figure.

FIGURE 13
Multiplying Measurements
When you multiply measurements, your answer can only have the same number of significant figures as the measurement with the fewest significant figures.

Multiplying or Dividing Measurements You need to follow a slightly different rule when you multiply or divide measurements. When multiplying or dividing, the answer can only have the same number of significant figures as the measurement with the fewest significant figures.

Suppose you need to tile a space that measures 2.25 meters by 3 meters. The area of the space would be calculated as follows:

$$\begin{array}{r} 2.25 \text{ m (3 signficant figures)} \\ \times\ 3 \text{ m (1 signficant figure)} \\ \hline 6.75 \text{ m}^2 = 7 \text{ m}^2 \text{ (1 significant figure)} \end{array}$$

The answer has one significant figure because the least precise measurement (3 meters) has one significant figure.

Reading Checkpoint What is the rule for multiplying or dividing measurements?

Percent Error

"Today, class, your job is to determine the density of this metal." With those words, your science teacher hands you a small piece of a shiny metal. You get to work, carefully measuring its mass and volume. When you divide the mass by the volume, you arrive at a density of 9.37 g/cm^3. "That's pretty close," says your teacher, "but now you need to calculate your percent error. The correct value for the density of this metal is 8.92 g/cm^3."

Percent error calculations are used to determine how accurate, or close to the true value, an experimental value really is. To calculate **percent error,** use the following formula:

$$\text{Percent error} = \frac{\text{Difference between experimental value and true value}}{\text{True value}} \times 100\%$$

A low percent error means that the result you obtained was very accurate. A high percent error means that your result was not very accurate. You may not have made your measurements carefully enough or your measurement tool may have been of poor quality.

Math Sample Problem

Percent Error
You calculate the density of an object to be 9.37 g/cm^3. The density of the object is actually 8.92 g/cm^3. Calculate your percent error.

1 Read and Understand
What information are you given?
Experimental value = 9.37 g/cm^3
True value = 8.92 g/cm^3

2 Plan and Solve
What quantity are you trying to calculate?
Percent error = ▪

What formula contains the given quantities and the unknown quantity?

$$\text{Percent Error} = \frac{\text{Difference between experimental value and true value}}{\text{True value}} \times 100\%$$

Perform the calculation.

$$\text{Percent error} = \frac{9.37 \text{ g/cm}^3 - 8.92 \text{ g/cm}^3}{8.92 \text{ g/cm}^3} \times 100\%$$

Percent error = 5.04%

3 Look Back and Check
Does your answer make sense?
The answer tells you that your percent error is about 5%. This answer makes sense because the experimental value and the true value were close to each other.

Math Practice

Tanya measured the mass of an object to be 187 g. Sam measured the object's mass to be 145 g. The object's actual mass was 170 g.

1. What is Tanya's percent error?

2. What is Sam's percent error?

FIGURE 14
Finding Mean, Median, and Mode
A green sea turtle can lay dozens of eggs at a time. The average number of eggs per nest can be expressed as a mean, median, or mode.

Mean, Median, and Mode

Walking along a beach one summer night, you spot a green sea turtle. The turtle has laid its eggs in the warm sand. How many eggs does a green sea turtle lay? Suppose you count the eggs and find that there are 107. Do all green sea turtles lay 107 eggs? To find out, you would have to study many more turtle nests.

Figure 14 shows data from a survey of green sea turtle nests on the beach. Notice that the number of eggs ranges from 94 to 110. How can you use this data to find the "average" number of eggs? **There are several ways to determine an "average." They include the mean, median, and mode.**

Mean One type of average is called the mean. The **mean,** or numerical average, is calculated by adding up all of the numbers and then dividing by the total number of items in the list.

$$\text{Mean} = \frac{\text{Sum of values}}{\text{Total number of values}}$$

Median Sometimes it may be more useful to know the **median,** or the middle number in a set of data. To find the median, place all the numbers in order from smallest to largest. If the ordered list has an odd number of entries, the median is the middle entry in the list. If a list has an even number of entries, you can find the median by adding the two middle numbers together and dividing by two.

Mode A third way to represent an average is called the mode. The **mode** is the number that appears most often in a list of numbers. The mode is particularly useful when a list contains many numbers that are the same.

 **Reading Checkpoint** What is the median number in a list that has an odd number of entries?

To Find the Mean

Add the numbers together and divide by the total number of items on the list.

Nest	Number of Eggs
A	110
B	102
C	94
D	110
E	107
F	110
G	109
Total	742

Mean = $\dfrac{742 \text{ eggs}}{7}$ = 106 eggs

To Find the Median

Place all the numbers in order from smallest to largest. The median is the middle entry.

94   102   107   (109)   110   110   110

Median = 109 eggs

To Find the Mode

Place all the numbers in order from smallest to largest. The mode is the number that appears most often.

94   102   107   109   (110   110   110)

Mode = 110 eggs

Section 2 Assessment

Target Reading Skill Asking Questions Work with a partner to check the answers about the section headings in your graphic organizer.

Reviewing Key Concepts

1. a. Identifying What math skill do scientists rely on when they cannot obtain exact numbers?
   b. Explaining Why is it important to obtain measurements that are both accurate and precise?
   c. Interpreting Data A friend measures the length of her room to be 3.7 meters. How many digits can you be certain of? Explain.
2. a. Listing What are three ways of calculating an "average"?
   b. Problem Solving Use all three ways to determine a student's "average" grade on eight exams: 88, 100, 92, 74, 90, 90, 84, 94.
   c. Calculating Suppose the student determined that his mean grade was 93. Calculate his percent error.

Math Practice

1. **Area** To win a prize at a fair, you must throw a coin into a space that is 7.0 cm long and 4.0 cm wide. What is the area of the space you are aiming for?

2. **Percent Error** You measured the cafeteria line to be 10.5 m long. The line is actually 6.2 m long. Calculate your percent error.

Graphs in Science

Reading Preview

Key Concepts
- What type of data can line graphs display?
- How do you determine a line of best fit or the slope of a graph?
- Why are line graphs powerful tools in science?

Key Terms
- graph • horizontal axis
- vertical axis • origin
- coordinate • data point
- line of best fit • linear graph
- slope • nonlinear graph

⊙ Target Reading Skill
Building Vocabulary A definition states the meaning of a word or phrase by telling about its most important feature or function. After you read this section, reread the paragraphs that contain definitions of Key Terms. Use all the information you have learned to write a definition of each Key Term in your own words.

Lab zone Discover **Activity**

What's in a Picture?
1. Read over the information written below.
2. At age 1, Sarah was 75 cm tall. By the time she turned 2, Sarah had grown 10 cm. By age 3, she had grown another 10 cm. At age 4, Sarah was 100 cm tall.
3. Look at the "picture" to the right.

Think It Over
Inferring What are the advantages of showing information in a visual way, rather than with words in paragraph form?

It's been a long day and all you can think about is food. You toss down your gym bag and head into the kitchen. Now for some pasta! You set a pot of water on the stove, turn on the heat, and wait eagerly for the water to boil.

Several minutes later, you are still waiting for the first sign of bubbles. Could the saying "A watched pot never boils" really be true? Or is the water taking longer to boil today because you filled the pot more than usual? Is the volume of water related to boiling time? You could do an experiment and collect some data to find out.

The Importance of Graphs

In Chapter 1, you learned why it is important to organize the data you collect in an experiment. Creating a data table is one way to organize experimental data. Another way to show data is in the form of a graph. You can think of a **graph** as a "picture" of your data. Have you ever heard the saying "A picture is worth a thousand words"? This is exactly why graphs are such useful tools. Because of their visual nature, graphs can reveal patterns or trends that words and data tables cannot.

The three types of graphs that scientists commonly use are bar graphs, circle graphs, and line graphs. You can learn about these graphs in the Skills Handbook. This section focuses specifically on line graphs—how to create them and how to interpret the patterns they reveal.

Why Are Line Graphs Useful? Suppose you set up the experiment in Figure 15. You record in a data table the time it takes each pot of water to boil. From your data table, you can tell that as the volume of water increases, the boiling time seems to increase as well. But a line graph could reveal more clearly how these two variables are related.

Line graphs are used to display data to show how one variable (the responding variable) changes in response to another variable (the manipulated variable). In the water-boiling experiment, the responding variable is the time it takes for the water to boil. The manipulated variable is the volume of water in the pot.

FIGURE 15
Collecting Data
How long does it take different volumes of water to boil? You can collect data and plot a line graph to see the relationship between volume and boiling time.
Inferring *Why might a line graph be more useful than a data table?*

Data Table	
Volume of Water (mL)	Boiling Time
500	7 min 48 s (7.8 min)
1,000	16 min 37 s (16.6 min)
1,500	26 min 00 s (26.0 min)
2,000	33 min 44 s (33.7 min)

Plotting a Line Graph When should you plot a line graph? The answer is, when your manipulated variable is *continuous*—that is, when there are other points between the ones that you tested. In the water-boiling experiment, volumes of 501 mL, 502 mL, and so on exist between 500 mL and 2,000 mL. Time and mass are other continuous variables.

To plot a line graph of your data, follow these steps.

1 Draw the axes. The **horizontal axis,** or *x*-axis, is the graph line that runs left to right. The **vertical axis,** or *y*-axis, is the graph line that runs up and down.

2 Label the axes. Label the horizontal axis with the name of the manipulated variable. Label the vertical axis with the name of the responding variable. Be sure to include units of measurement on each axis.

3 Create a scale. On each axis, create a scale by marking off equally-spaced intervals that cover the range of values you will show. Both scales should begin at zero when possible. The point where the two axes cross is called the **origin** of the graph. On this graph, the origin has coordinates of (0,0), which represents "0 milliliters and 0 minutes." A **coordinate** is a pair of numbers used to determine the position of a point on a graph.

4 Plot the data. Plot a point for each piece of data. The dotted lines show how to plot your first piece of data (500, 7.8). Follow an imaginary vertical line extending up from the horizontal axis at the 500 mL mark. Then follow an imaginary horizontal line extending across from the vertical axis at the 7.8 minutes mark. Plot a point where these two lines cross, or intersect. The point showing the location of that intersection is called a **data point.**

5 Draw a "line of best fit." A **line of best fit** is a smooth line that reflects the general pattern of a graph. Though your first instinct might be to simply connect all the dots, that's not the correct approach to drawing a line graph. Rather, you should first stop and look at the points you plotted to identify a general trend in the data. Then draw a smooth line between the points to reflect that general pattern.

Notice that the resulting line of best fit for this graph is a straight line. A line graph in which the data points yield a straight line is called a **linear graph.**

6 Add a title that identifies the variables or relationship shown in the graph.

Data Table	
Volume of Water (mL)	Boiling Time (min)
500	7.8
1,000	16.6
1,500	26.0
2,000	33.7

Reading Checkpoint What is a data point?

FIGURE 16

Plotting a Line Graph

You can obtain a picture of your experimental data by following these six steps.

Go Online
active art

For: Plotting a line graph activity
Visit: PHSchool.com
Web Code: cgp-6023

1 Draw the Axes

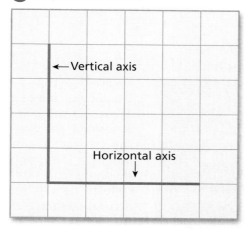

← Vertical axis

Horizontal axis
↓

2 Label the Axes

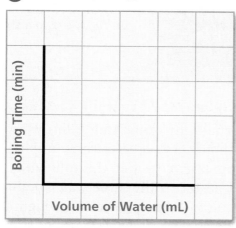

Boiling Time (min)

Volume of Water (mL)

3 Create a Scale

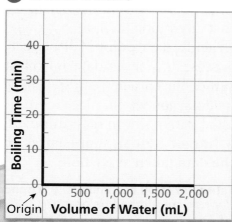

Boiling Time (min)

Origin   Volume of Water (mL)

4 Plot the Data

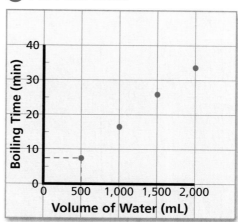

5 Draw a Line of Best Fit

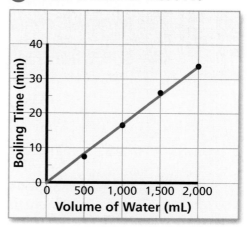

6 Add a Title

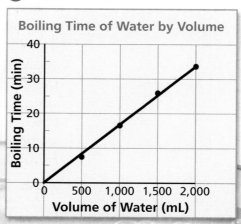

Boiling Time of Water by Volume

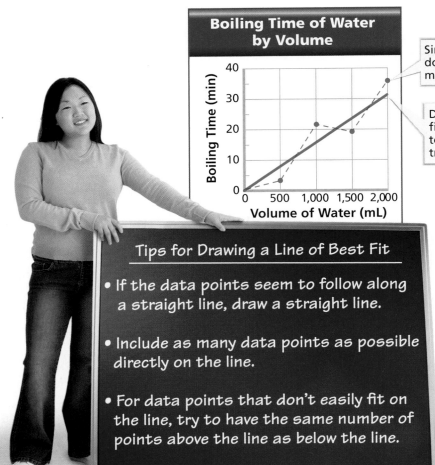

Boiling Time of Water by Volume

Simply connecting the dots is incorrect and may be misleading.

Drawing a line of best fit is the proper way to reflect the overall trend in the data.

Tips for Drawing a Line of Best Fit

- If the data points seem to follow along a straight line, draw a straight line.

- Include as many data points as possible directly on the line.

- For data points that don't easily fit on the line, try to have the same number of points above the line as below the line.

FIGURE 17
Drawing a Line of Best Fit
These tips will help you determine the overall trend shown by your experimental data. For this graph, a line going up from left to right reflects the data more accurately than a zigzag line does.
Relating Cause and Effect
What factors might explain why the data points don't fall perfectly along a straight line?

Why Draw a Line of Best Fit?

You may be wondering why you cannot simply connect all your data points with a line to create a line graph. To understand why this is the case, consider the following situation. Suppose your friend performs the same water-boiling experiment as you did and plots the graph shown in Figure 17.

Notice that your friend's graph shows the same general trend as yours—points going upwards from left to right. However, if your friend simply connects the dots, the line would be a zigzag, rather than a straight line.

Why don't your friend's data points fall perfectly along a straight line? It is because whenever data is collected, small measurement errors and inaccuracies can be introduced. By simply connecting the dots, you would place too much importance on each individual data point in determining the overall shape of the line. **A line of best fit emphasizes the overall trend shown by all the data taken as a whole.**

 **Reading Checkpoint** Why shouldn't you automatically "connect the dots" when creating a line graph?

Slope

When a line graph is linear, you can determine a value called slope. One way to define **slope** is the steepness of the graph line. **The slope of a graph line tells you how much y changes for every change in x.** Thus, another definition of slope is the ratio of the vertical change (the "rise") to the horizontal change (the "run"). Slope is calculated using this formula:

$$\text{Slope} = \frac{\text{Rise}}{\text{Run}} = \frac{Y_2 - Y_1}{X_2 - X_1}$$

To calculate slope, pick any two points on the line and write down the coordinates. In Figure 18, suppose you chose the points $(20, 10)$ and $(50, 25)$.

$$\text{Slope} = \frac{25\ \text{km} - 10\ \text{km}}{50\ \text{min} - 20\ \text{min}} = \frac{15\ \text{km}}{30\ \text{min}} = 0.5\ \text{km/min}$$

In the case of Figure 18, the slope represents the distance the car travels per unit of time, or its speed. A slope of 0.5 tells you that the car has a speed of 0.5 km/min.

✓ **Reading Checkpoint** What are two ways to define slope?

FIGURE 18
Slope
The slope of a line indicates how much y changes for every change in x. **Calculating** *What is the slope of this line?*

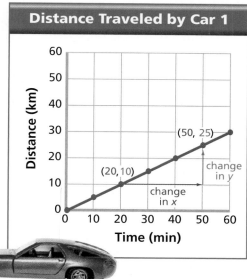

Distance Traveled by Car 1

Math ► Analyzing Data

Car Travel

The graph shows the distance a car travels in a one-hour period. Use the graph to answer the questions below.

1. **Reading Graphs** What variable is plotted on the horizontal axis? What variable is plotted on the vertical axis?

2. **Interpreting Data** How far does the car travel in the first 10 minutes? In 40 minutes?

3. **Predicting** Use the graph to predict how far the car would travel in 120 minutes. Assume the car continues to travel at the same speed.

4. **Calculating** Calculate the slope of the graph. What information does the slope provide about the speed of Car 2?

5. **Drawing Conclusions** Compare this graph to the one for Car 1 in Figure 18. What is the relationship between the steepness of the graph lines and the speed of the cars?

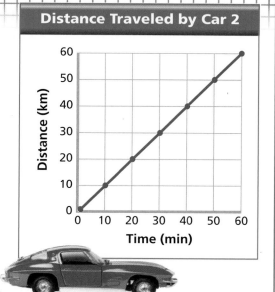

Distance Traveled by Car 2

FIGURE 19
Trends in Graphs

Data may yield one of the trends shown in these graphs.

Reading Graphs *Which graph shows no relationship between the two variables?*

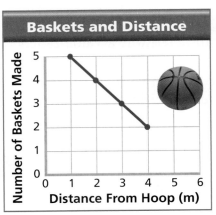

Baskets and Distance

Number of Baskets Made vs. Distance From Hoop (m)

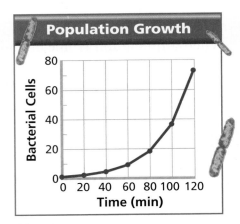

Population Growth

Bacterial Cells vs. Time (min)

A **Linear Trend** As the distance from the hoop increases, the number of baskets made decreases. The graph line descends to the right.

B **Nonlinear Trend** Bacteria reproduce by dividing in two every 20 minutes. The number of bacterial cells increases sharply. The graph is a steep curve.

Using Graphs to Identify Trends

Your data won't always give you a graph with a straight line. A line graph in which the data points do not fall along a straight line is called a **nonlinear graph.**

Whether a graph is linear or nonlinear, the information it contains is very useful. **Line graphs are powerful tools in science because they allow you to identify trends and make predictions.**

Linear Trends When a graph is linear, you can easily see how two variables are related. For instance, Graph A in Figure 19 shows that the farther one student stands from a basketball hoop, the fewer baskets she can make.

You can also use the graph to make predictions. For example, how many baskets can she make at a distance of 5 meters? If you extend the graph line, you can see that your prediction would be one basket.

Nonlinear Trends There are several kinds of nonlinear graphs. In some nonlinear graphs, the data points may fall along a curve. A curve may be shallow, or it may be steep, as in Graph B.

Other nonlinear graphs show different trends. A graph may rise and then level off, as in Graph C. Or, a graph may show a repeating pattern, as in Graph D. Because each of these graphs reveals a trend in the data, they are useful in understanding how the variables are related.

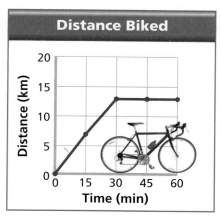

Distance Biked

Distance (km) vs. Time (min)

C **Nonlinear Trend** On a bike ride, the distance you bike increases with time. If you stop to rest, the distance remains the same and the graph levels off.

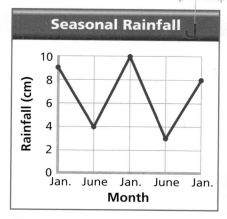

Seasonal Rainfall

Rainfall (cm) vs. Month

D **Nonlinear Trend** In many places, rainfall varies with the seasons. The graph shows a repeating, or cyclical, pattern.

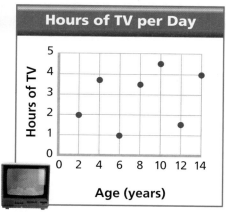

Hours of TV per Day

Hours of TV vs. Age (years)

E **No Trend** The amount of television children watch and their ages are not related. The data points are scattered, and the graph shows no recognizable pattern.

No Trend In other nonlinear graphs, the data points may be scattered about in no recognizable pattern, as in Graph E. Would you be surprised to learn that even such graphs are useful? When there are no identifiable trends in a graph, it most likely means that there is no relationship between the two variables.

Reading Checkpoint What is a nonlinear graph?

Section 3 Assessment

Target Reading Skill Building Vocabulary Use your definitions to help answer the questions below.

Reviewing Key Concepts

1. a. Reviewing What can graphs reveal that data tables cannot?
  b. Describing What can a line graph tell you about the relationship between the variables in an experiment?
  c. Interpreting Data Could you use a line graph to show data about how body mass (the responding variable) changes with height (the manipulated variable)? Explain.

2. a. Defining What is a line of best fit?
  b. Explaining What does calculating the slope of a graph line tell you about the data?
  c. Comparing and Contrasting How does a graph line with a steeper slope compare to one with a shallower slope?

3. a. Listing List two things that line graphs allow scientists to do.
  b. Reading Graphs Describe how Graph D in Figure 19 allows scientists to do these two things.

Lab zone **At-Home Activity**

Which Line Is Best? Show a family member how to "draw" a line of best fit by plotting the data points from Figure 17 onto a piece of graph paper. Tape the graph paper onto a thick piece of cardboard. Insert a pushpin into each data point. Then arrange a piece of string so that it best reflects the data. Once you have determined the line of best fit, tape the string to the graph. Explain why a line of best fit need not go through each data point.

Go Online
PHSchool.com

For: Data sharing
Visit: PHSchool.com
Web Code: cgd-6023

Density Graphs

Problem
How can you determine the density of a liquid?

Skills Focus
graphing, calculating

Materials
• graduated cylinder • balance
• graph paper • 3 samples of a liquid

Procedure

1. Measure the mass of an empty graduated cylinder. Record the mass in a data table.

2. Pour one of the liquid samples into the graduated cylinder. Measure and record the mass of the graduated cylinder plus the liquid.

3. Calculate the mass of the liquid alone by subtracting the mass of the empty graduated cylinder from the mass in Step 2.

4. Determine the volume of the liquid by reading the level at the bottom of the meniscus.

5. Repeat Steps 2–4 with the two other samples.

Analyze and Conclude

1. **Graphing** Use the data in your data table to create a graph. Graph volume on the horizontal axis and mass on the vertical axis.

2. **Interpreting Data** Look at the points you plotted to identify a general trend in the data. Then draw a line of best fit that reflects the trend in the data.

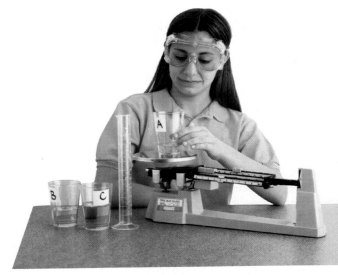

3. **Calculating** Select two points along the graph line and use them to calculate the slope of the line. Use this formula:

$$\text{Slope} = \frac{\text{Rise}}{\text{Run}} = \frac{Y_2 - Y_1}{X_2 - X_1}$$

4. **Drawing Conclusions** Explain why the slope represents the density of the liquid.

5. **Communicating** In a paragraph, explain why mass and volume measurements for any sample of the liquid should fall along the graph line.

Design an Experiment
Propose a plan to determine which is more dense—a marble or the liquid you used in this lab. *Obtain your teacher's permission before carrying out your investigation.*

Data Table				
Sample	Mass of Empty Graduated Cylinder	Mass of Liquid and Graduated Cylinder	Mass of Liquid Alone	Volume of Liquid
1				
2				
3				

Safety in the Science Laboratory

Reading Preview

Key Concepts
- Why is preparation important when carrying out scientific investigations in the lab and in the field?
- What should you do if an accident occurs?

Target Reading Skill
Outlining As you read, make an outline about science safety that you can use for review. Use the red headings for the main ideas and the blue headings for supporting ideas.

Safety in the Science Laboratory
I. Safety in the lab
A. Preparing for the lab
B.
C.
II. Safety in the field

Where Is the Safety Equipment in Your School?

1. Look around your classroom or school for any safety-related equipment.
2. Draw a floor plan of the room or building and clearly label where each item is located.

Think It Over
Predicting Why is it important to know where safety equipment is located?

After hiking for a few hours, your group finally reaches a beautiful campsite by a lake. Your first task is to set up tents. Eager to explore the area, you toss aside the tent directions, thinking to yourself, "How hard could it be?" You begin to put all the pieces together, guessing as you go. When you have finished, you step back to survey your work. You notice that the tent is quite lopsided. Deciding that it will do, you run off with your friends to explore.

Later that night, as you settle into your sleeping bag, heavy rain starts to fall. Water begins to pour in through the lopsided part of the tent. You look for a flashlight so you can investigate. But then you realize that you forgot to pack one.

You have probably heard the motto, "Be prepared." Obviously, following that advice would have been helpful in this situation. Proper preparation for the camping trip should have included reading the tent directions and packing the proper supplies. The result would probably have been a more enjoyable camping experience.

Safety in the Lab

Just as when you go camping, you have to be prepared before you begin any scientific investigation. **Good preparation helps you stay safe when doing science activities in the laboratory.**

Thermometers, balances, and glassware—these are some of the equipment you will use in science labs. Do you know how to use these items? What should you do if something goes wrong? Thinking about these questions ahead of time is an important part of being prepared.

Preparing for the Lab Preparing for a lab should begin the day before you will perform the lab. It is important to read through the procedure carefully and make sure you understand all the directions. Also, review the general safety guidelines in Appendix A, including those related to the specific equipment you will use. If anything is unclear, be prepared to ask your teacher about it before you begin the lab.

FIGURE 20
Safety in the Lab
Good preparation for an experiment helps you stay safe in the laboratory. **Observing** *List three precautions each student is taking while performing the labs.*

Performing the Lab Whenever you perform a science lab, your chief concern must be the safety of yourself, your classmates, and your teacher. The most important safety rule is simple: Always follow your teacher's instructions and the textbook directions exactly. You should never try anything on your own without asking your teacher first.

Labs and activities in this textbook series include safety symbols such as those at right. These symbols alert you to possible dangers in performing the lab and remind you to work carefully. They also identify any safety equipment that you should use to protect yourself from potential hazards. The symbols are explained in detail in Appendix A. Make sure you are familiar with each safety symbol and what it means.

Other things you can do to make your lab experience safe and successful include keeping your work area clean and organized. Also, do not rush through any of the steps. Finally, always show respect and courtesy to your teacher and classmates.

Safety Symbols

 Safety Goggles

 Lab Apron

 Breakage

 Heat-Resistant Gloves

 Plastic Gloves

 Heating

 Flames

 No Flames

 Corrosive Chemical

 Poison

 Fumes

 Sharp Object

 Animal Safety

 Plant Safety

 Electric Shock

 Physical Safety

 Disposal

 Hand Washing

 General Safety Awareness

Wear plastic gloves to protect your skin when handling animals, plants, or chemicals.

Handle live animals and plants with care.

Tie back long hair to keep it away from flames, chemicals, or equipment.

End-of-Lab Procedures Your lab work does not end when you reach the last step in the procedure. There are important things you need to do at the end of every lab.

When you have completed a lab, be sure to clean up your work area. Turn off and unplug any equipment and return it to its proper place. It is very important that you dispose of any waste materials properly. Some wastes should not be thrown in the trash or poured down the drain. Follow your teacher's instructions about proper disposal. Finally, be sure to wash your hands thoroughly after working in the laboratory.

Safety in the Field

The laboratory is not the only place where you will conduct scientific investigations. Some investigations will be done in the "field." The field can be any outdoor area, such as a schoolyard, a forest, a park, or a beach. **Just as in the laboratory, good preparation helps you stay safe when doing science activities in the field.**

There can be many potential safety hazards outdoors. For example, you could encounter severe weather, traffic, wild animals, or poisonous plants. Advance planning may help you avoid some potential hazards. For example, you can listen to the weather forecast and plan your trip accordingly. Other hazards may be impossible to anticipate.

Whenever you do field work, always tell an adult where you will be. Never carry out a field investigation alone. Ask an adult or a classmate to accompany you. Dress appropriately for the weather and other conditions you will encounter. Use common sense to avoid any potentially dangerous situations.

 **What are some potential outdoor hazards?**

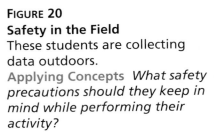
FIGURE 20
Safety in the Field
These students are collecting data outdoors.
Applying Concepts *What safety precautions should they keep in mind while performing their activity?*

In Case of an Accident

Good preparation and careful work habits can go a long way toward making your lab experiences safe ones. But, at some point, an accident may occur. A classmate might accidentally knock over a beaker or a chemical might spill on your sleeve. Would you know what to do?

When any accident occurs, no matter how minor, notify your teacher immediately. Then, listen to your teacher's directions and carry them out quickly. Make sure you know the location and proper use of all the emergency equipment in your lab room. Knowing safety and first aid procedures beforehand will prepare you to handle accidents properly. Figure 22 lists some first-aid procedures you should know.

 **What should you do when an accident occurs?**

In Case of Emergency

ALWAYS NOTIFY YOUR TEACHER IMMEDIATELY

Injury	What to Do
Burns	Immerse burns in cold water.
Cuts	Cover cuts with a clean dressing. Apply direct pressure to the wound to stop bleeding.
Spills on Skin	Flush the skin with large amounts of water.
Foreign Object in Eye	Flush the eye with large amounts of water. Seek medical attention.

FIGURE 22
First-Aid Tips
These first-aid tips can help guide your actions during emergency situations. Remember, always notify your teacher immediately if an accident occurs.

Section 4 Assessment

Target Reading Skill Outlining Use the information in your outline about science safety to help you answer the questions below.

Reviewing Key Concepts

1. a. Listing List two things you should do ahead of time to prepare for a lab.

   b. Interpreting Diagrams Suppose a lab included the safety symbols below. What do these symbols mean? What precautions should you take?

   c. Making Generalizations Why is it more difficult to prepare for a lab activity in the field than for one in a laboratory?

2. a. Reviewing Suppose during a lab activity you get a cut and start to bleed. What is the first thing you should do?

   b. Sequencing Outline in order the next steps you would take to deal with your injury.

   c. Making Judgments Some people feel that most accidents that occur really could have been prevented with better preparation or safer behaviors. Do you agree or disagree with this viewpoint? Explain your reasoning.

Writing in Science

Safety Poster Make a poster of one of the safety rules in Appendix A to post in your lab. Be sure to include the safety symbol, clear directions, and additional illustrations.

Study Guide

① Measurement—A Common Language

Key Concepts

- Using SI as the standard system of measurement allows scientists to compare data and communicate with each other about their results.

- SI units of measure include the meter (length), kilogram (mass), cubic meter (volume), kilograms per cubic meter (density), second (time), and Kelvin (temperature).

- Volume = Length × Width × Height

- Density $= \dfrac{\text{Mass}}{\text{Volume}}$

- To convert one measurement to another, you need to know the appropriate conversion factor. A conversion factor is an equation that shows how two units of measurement are related.

Key Terms

metric system	weight	density
SI	volume	
mass	meniscus	

② Mathematics and Science

Key Concepts

- In collecting data and making measurements, scientists use math skills involving estimation, accuracy and precision, and significant figures.

- When analyzing data, scientists use math skills involving percent error, mean, median, and mode.

- Percent error $= \dfrac{\text{Difference between experimental value and true value}}{\text{True value}} \times 100\%$

- Mean $= \dfrac{\text{Sum of values}}{\text{Total number of values}}$

Key Terms

estimate	percent error
accuracy	mean
precision	median
significant figures	mode

③ Graphs in Science

Key Concepts

- Line graphs are used to display data to see how one variable (the responding variable) changes in response to another variable (the manipulated variable).

- A line of best fit emphasizes the overall trend shown by all the data taken as a whole.

- The slope of a graph line tells you how much y changes for every change in x.

$$\text{Slope} = \frac{\text{Rise}}{\text{Run}} = \frac{Y_2 - Y_1}{X_2 - X_1}$$

- Line graphs are powerful tools in science because they allow you to identify trends and make predictions.

Key Terms

graph
horizontal axis
vertical axis
origin
coordinate
data point
line of best fit
linear graph
slope
nonlinear graph

④ Safety in the Science Laboratory

Key Concepts

- Good preparation helps you stay safe when doing science activities in the laboratory.

- Just as in the laboratory, good preparation helps you stay safe when doing science activities in the field.

- When any accident occurs, no matter how minor, notify your teacher immediately. Then, listen to your teacher's directions and carry them out quickly.

Review and Assessment

Organizing Information

Concept Mapping Copy the concept map about averages onto a separate sheet of paper. Then complete it and add a title. (For more on Concept Mapping, see the Skills Handbook.)

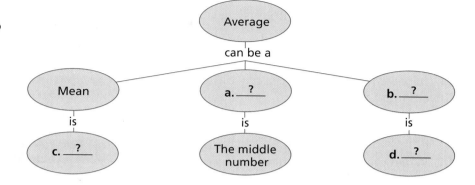

Reviewing Key Terms

Choose the letter of the best answer.

1. The amount of matter an object contains is its
   a. length.   b. mass.
   c. weight.   d. volume.

2. The significant figures in a measurement
   a. include only the first two digits.
   b. include only the estimated digits.
   c. include only the digits that have been measured exactly.
   d. include all of the digits that have been measured exactly, plus one digit.

3. Percent error calculations are used to determine
   a. the distance from one point to another.
   b. how accurate an experimental value is.
   c. how precise an experimental value is.
   d. the steepness of a graph line.

4. The median of a set of numbers is
   a. an estimate.
   b. the middle number.
   c. the numerical average.
   d. the number that appears most often.

5. The point where the *x*-axis and the *y*-axis cross on a graph is called the
   a. origin.
   b. coordinate.
   c. meniscus.
   d. variable.

If the statement is true, write *true*. If it is false, change the underlined word or words to make the statement true.

6. The basic SI unit of length is the <u>gram</u>.

7. A common unit of <u>volume</u> is g/cm^3.

8. <u>Precision</u> refers to how close a measurement is to the true or accepted value.

9. The horizontal axis on a graph is also known as the <u>*x*-axis</u>.

10. The <u>slope</u> of a graph line tells you how much *y* changes for every change in *x*.

Writing in Science

Interview You are a sports reporter interviewing an Olympic swimmer who lost the silver medal by a few hundredths of a second. Write a one page interview in which you discuss the meaning of time and the advanced instruments used to measure time.

The Work of Scientists
Video Preview
Video Field Trip
► Video Assessment

Review and Assessment

Checking Concepts

11. Why must scientists use standard units of measure in their experiments?

12. In your own words, describe the difference between mass and weight.

13. In what ways do scientists rely on mathematics in their work?

14. Why is it important to be both accurate and precise when you make measurements?

15. When graphing, why should you draw a smooth line that reflects the general pattern, rather than automatically connect the data points?

16. List three things you can do to prepare for a lab experiment.

Thinking Critically

17. **Comparing and Contrasting** Which of the objects below has a greater volume? Explain.

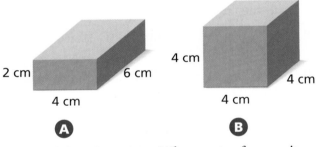

18. **Applying Concepts** When water freezes, it expands. Use this statement and your knowledge of density to explain why ice cubes float in water.

19. **Relating Cause and Effect** In a lab activity that involves many measurements and calculations, you and your lab partner rush through the procedures. In the end, you obtain a percent error of 50 percent. Explain what may have led to such a high percent error.

20. **Making Judgments** Why do you think that, as a general precaution, you should never bring food or drink into a laboratory?

Math Practice

21. **Calculating Density** A 12.5 g marble displaces 5 mL of water. What is its density?

22. **Area** Calculate the area of a picture frame that measures 17 cm × 12 cm.

23. **Percent Error** You measure the mass of a mystery object to be 658 g. The actual mass of the object is 755 g. What is your percent error?

Applying Skills

Use the graph to answer Questions 24–26.

A scientist measured the distance a lava stream flowed over 5 minutes.

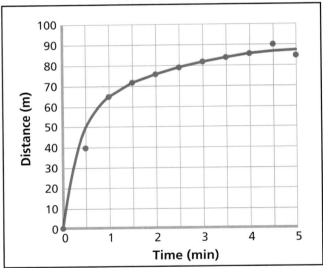

24. **Reading Graphs** What is plotted on each axis?

25. **Interpreting Data** Did the stream travel the same distance every minute? Explain.

26. **Predicting** Predict the movement of the stream between 5 and 6 minutes.

Lab zone Chapter **Project**

Performance Assessment Display your model and explain how you chose its scale. What was the most difficult thing about creating your model to scale? How could you improve your model?

Standardized Test Prep

Choose the letter of the best answer.

1. A student grows tomatoes for an experiment. Which piece of equipment will he need to determine the mass of the tomatoes?
   A graduated cylinder
   B meter stick
   C bathroom scale
   D triple-beam balance

2. Ranida measured the length of a string several times and obtained these measurements: 21.5 cm, 21.3 cm, 21.7 cm, and 21.6 cm. The actual length of the string is 25.5 cm. Which of the following statements best describes Ranida's measurements?
   F The measurements were accurate.
   G The measurements were not accurate, but they were precise.
   H The measurements were both accurate and precise.
   J The measurements were neither accurate nor precise.

3. Ellis measured the mass of five samples of quartz. His results were 39.75 g, 38.91 g, 37.66 g, 39.75 g, and 39.55 g. What was the mean mass of the samples?
   A 39.55 g   **B** 39.75 g
   C 38.91 g   **D** 39.12 g

The graph below shows the masses of five different volumes of liquid. Use the graph and your knowledge of science to answer Questions 4–5.

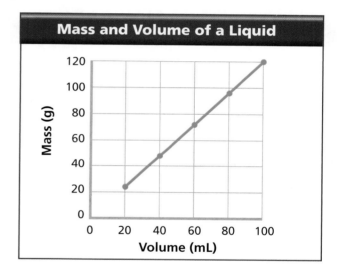

4. What is the general trend in the data?
   F There is no trend in the data.
   G There is a linear trend in the data.
   H There is a nonlinear trend in the data.
   J The trend is linear at first but then becomes nonlinear.

5. What is the slope of the graph line?
   A −1.0 g/mL   **B** 1.0 g/mL
   C 1.2 mL/g   **D** 1.2 g/mL

Constructed Response

6. Two students arrive at science class before anyone else. They want to finish the day's lab early and decide to begin the experiment. The first step involves heating a beaker of water. The students set up a hot plate near the sink to be close to the water. They fill the beaker with water and set the wet beaker onto the hot plate. Identify all the things the students did wrong and why.

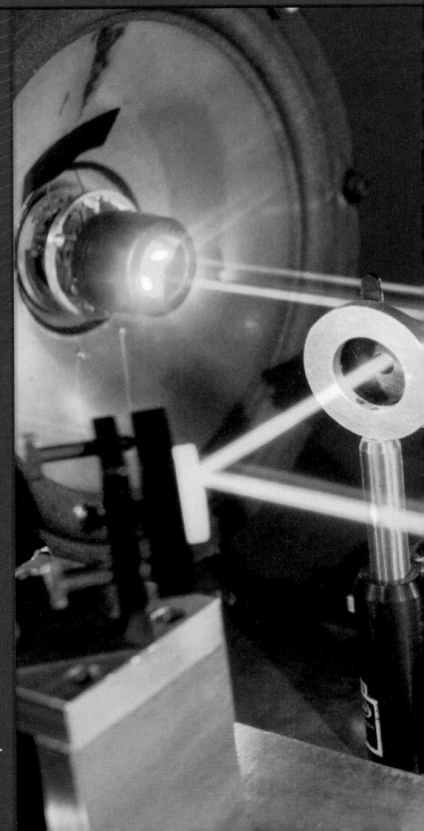

Chapter

3

Technology and Engineering

Chapter Preview

interactive Textbook

Lasers are used in many technology products, ▶
from supermarket scanners to audio equipment.

Lab zone™ Chapter **Project**

Design and Build a Chair

Do you have a favorite chair? If so, what makes it more comfortable than the desk chairs at school? The answer lies in its design. In this chapter project, you will explore the process by which a chair is designed and built.

Your Goal To design and build a chair made of cardboard

The chair you build must

- be constructed from no more than 4 square meters of cardboard
- have a seat and a sturdy back
- support at least 20 kilograms of books
- be built following the safety guidelines in Appendix A

Plan It! Examine several chairs to see how they are built. Observe how the chair parts are joined together. Preview the chapter to learn more about the technology design process. Then sketch your chair design. When your teacher has approved your design, start to build your chair.

Understanding Technology

Reading Preview

Key Concepts
- What is the goal of technology?
- How does technology differ from science?
- What factors cause technology to progress?
- What are the components of a technological system?

Key Terms
- technology • obsolete
- system • goal • input
- process • output • feedback

Target Reading Skill
Previewing Visuals When you preview, you look ahead at the material to be read. Preview Figure 3. Then write two questions you have about the diagram in a graphic organizer like the one below. As you read, answer your questions.

Science and Technology

Q.	What does technology have to do with science?
A.	
Q.	

Lab zone Discover **Activity**

What Are Some Examples of Technology?
1. Look at the objects in the photographs.
2. With a partner, discuss whether or not each object is an example of technology. Write your reasons for each decision.

Think It Over
Forming Operational Definitions On what basis did you and your partner decide whether an object was an example of technology? What is your definition of *technology*?

The year is 1900, and you are going to visit your aunt and uncle in a distant city. You awaken before dawn and get dressed by the flickering light of an oil lamp. Then you and your family hurry to the train station. The train ride is quite an experience. You never imagined anything could move so fast.

Your aunt and uncle greet you with hot soup prepared on their shiny, black, coal-burning stove. After the meal, you help with the cleanup. As you wash the bowls and spoons, you are amazed by the water faucet. To get water at home, you must go outside and pump it by hand.

FIGURE 1
Technology Through the Decades
The products shown in these ads are examples of technology. Although they may seem outdated, they were sensations in their time!

Phonograph: 1900s ▶

What Is Technology?

Trains, coal-burning stoves, and water faucets all made life easier for people living in 1900. So did oil lamps and water pumps, even though they may seem old-fashioned. All of these items are examples of technology. In fact, even bowls and spoons are forms of technology. But what does *technology* mean?

Meanings of Technology When you see or hear the word *technology*, you may think of things such as computers, CD players, and cellphones. But technology includes more than modern inventions. Ancient inventions, such as stone tools, the wheel, and the compass, are examples of technology, too. Technology has been around since people started to make things to suit their needs.

In addition to things that people make, technology can also refer to the knowledge and processes needed to produce those objects. Put simply, **technology** is how people change the world around them to meet their needs or to solve practical problems.

▲ Automobile: 1920s

▲ Washing machine: 1950s

▲ Television: 1960s

Classifying

Look around you. Write down one example of each of the six areas of technology. Compare your list with a classmate's. Discuss any items on your lists that you classified differently.

The Goal of Technology What is the purpose of technology? **The goal of technology is to improve the way people live.** Think about the many ways that technology has improved people's lives. Medicines help you recover from sickness. Eyeglasses and binoculars extend your ability to see. The Internet makes it easier for you to obtain information.

Areas of Technology The products of technology can be classified into six major areas, which are shown in Figure 2. You probably use technology products from each of these areas every day.

Although the six areas of technology may seem distinct, they are not separate. For example, think about all the technologies involved in bringing a box of cereal to your breakfast table. Trains (transportation) carry grain from farms to factories (construction). There, vitamins and minerals (biological and chemical) are added to the grain. The cereal is baked in an oven (energy and power) and then packaged in plastic bags and cardboard boxes (manufacturing). Trucks transport the boxes to supermarkets, while the cereal company advertises the product on TV (communication). Finally, you buy the cereal and enjoy it for breakfast.

FIGURE 2
Areas of Technology
Technology can be classified into six major areas. If you've ever gone camping, you've probably relied on products from all six areas. In fact, almost everything you do involves products from the different areas of technology.

Reading Checkpoint **What is an example of transportation technology?**

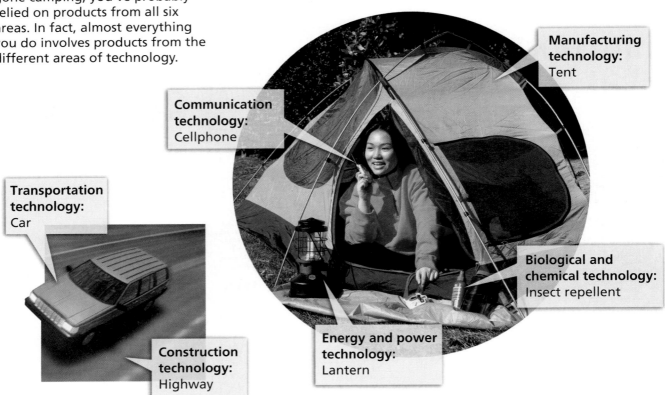

Communication technology: Cellphone

Manufacturing technology: Tent

Transportation technology: Car

Biological and chemical technology: Insect repellent

Construction technology: Highway

Energy and power technology: Lantern

Science

Scientists learn how light moves through substances.

Technology

Engineers develop optical fibers, thin tubes that carry light. Optical fibers are used in communication networks and medicine.

Science

Doctors use optical fibers to learn more about how the heart functions.

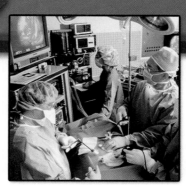

How Does Technology Relate to Science?

You might wonder why you are learning about technology in a science book. Are science and technology the same thing? The answer is no. In fact, the purposes of science and technology are quite different. **Science is the study of the natural world to understand how it functions. Technology, on the other hand, changes, or modifies, the natural world to meet human needs or solve problems.**

To make the difference clear, contrast how scientists and technologists might view air currents, or winds. A scientist might study how air currents develop and how they affect weather conditions. A technologist, in contrast, might study how wind can be harnessed to produce electricity. In other words, a scientist studies something to learn about the topic itself. A technologist studies a topic to learn how people can apply that knowledge to solve problems.

Often, advances in science and technology depend on one another, as shown in Figure 3. Endoscopes are tiny medical instruments that allow doctors to view organs within the human body. Endoscopes transmit light using long, thin strands of glass called optical fibers. The design of these fibers would not have been possible without the work of scientists. Once scientists understood how light travels through substances, technologists were able to use this knowledge to design optical fibers and endoscopes. Endoscopes, in turn, have helped scientists learn more about the human body.

FIGURE 3
Science and Technology
Advances in science contribute to advances in technology, which in turn contribute to science. Understanding the physics of light (science) led to the development of optical fibers and endoscopes (technology).
Relating Cause and Effect *How might endoscopes help scientists learn more about the human body?*

 **Reading Checkpoint** What might a technologist study about wind?

How Technology Progresses

Technology is always changing. Suppose a technological product, such as your CD player, breaks and you shop for a new one. Chances are good that you will find a new system that is better than your old one. Perhaps it will be smaller or easier to use. **Technology progresses as people's knowledge increases and as new needs can be satisfied.**

Obsolete Technologies A product may become **obsolete,** or no longer used. A technology becomes obsolete if it no longer meets people's needs as well as newer products do. Consider manual typewriters, for instance. Manual typewriters were quite useful in their time, but they had disadvantages. For example, they were noisy, and it was difficult to make changes to the typed document. Eventually, manual typewriters were replaced by electronic versions. Typewriters still exist today, but most people use computers with word processing programs instead.

Current Technologies Word processing programs are one example of a current technology. Current technologies are those in use at the present time. Word processing programs meet human needs because they perform more functions than typewriters, such as saving documents. In addition, they are easier to use. Reorganizing text, for example, is much easier with word processed documents than with typed documents.

FIGURE 4
The Progress of Technology

Today, manual typewriters are obsolete and have been replaced by computers with word processing programs. At the same time, voice recognition software is an emerging new technology. Pens and pencils coexist with these newer technologies.
Making Judgments *Do you think that pens and pencils will ever become obsolete? Why or why not?*

Obsolete Technology   **Current Technology**

Emerging Technologies Imagine writing an essay just by speaking into a microphone. As you speak, the words show up on your computer screen. Computer software that can recognize and process human voices is an emerging technology. Emerging technologies are those that are just beginning to become widely available. People commonly refer to complex emerging technologies as high technology, or "high tech."

Because emerging technologies are so new, they may be expensive and may not yet work perfectly. For example, voice recognition software may not be able to distinguish between words that sound alike, such as *choose* and *chews*.

Over time, emerging technologies usually improve and become less expensive. Technologies that are new and revolutionary today may be a normal part of life in a few years. When this happens, they become current technologies.

Coexisting Technologies Not all old technologies become obsolete and get replaced by emerging technologies. Some old technologies, such as pens and pencils, coexist along with current ones because they still fulfill people's needs. An older, simpler form of a technology may be more useful in certain situations than a current product. On a camping trip, for example, a hand-operated can opener is more useful than an electric one!

 **Reading Checkpoint** What is meant by "emerging technology"?

Lab zone Try This Activity

Progress Report
In this activity, you will learn how a certain technology has changed over time.

1. Talk with an older adult about the technologies they used to listen to music in the past.
2. Create a "timeline" similar to the one in Figure 4 identifying music technologies that are obsolete, current, emerging, and coexisting.

Predicting How do you think music technology will change during your lifetime?

Emerging Technology

Coexisting Technology

To team members

Memo: To team members

FIGURE 5
The Oven as a System

An oven is a technological system. Input, process, output, and feedback are all involved in achieving the goal of cooking food—such as tasty cookies!

Goal

Bake a tray of chocolate chip cookies.

Inputs

- Gas is turned on.
- Temperature is set.
- Tray of raw cookie dough is put in.

Processes

Burning gas causes the oven chamber to heat up.

Outputs

- Heat is released.
- Temperature reaches set level.
- Cookies bake.

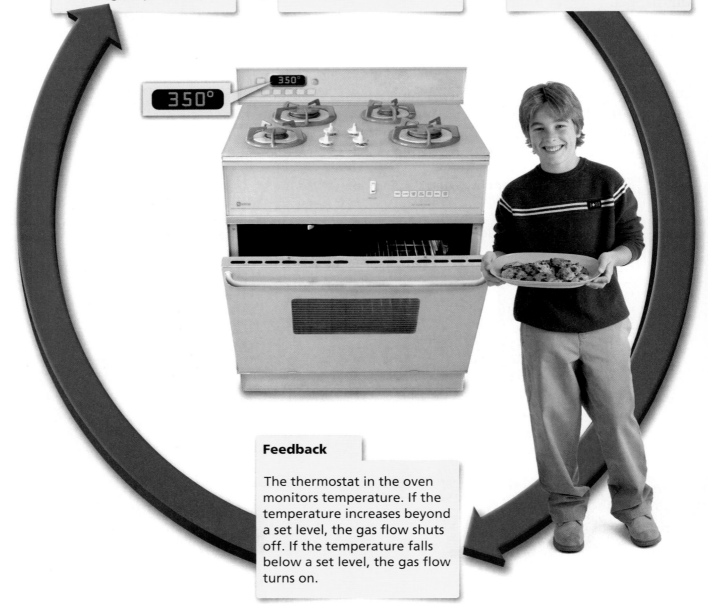

Feedback

The thermostat in the oven monitors temperature. If the temperature increases beyond a set level, the gas flow shuts off. If the temperature falls below a set level, the gas flow turns on.

Technology as a System

When you hear the word *system*, what comes to mind? Maybe you think of your school system or the circulatory system in your body. All **systems** have one thing in common: They are made of parts that work together. The parts of your school system include buildings, books, and teachers. All of these parts are involved in educating the students in your community.

Technology products can be thought of as systems, too. **A technological system includes a goal, inputs, processes, outputs, and, in some cases, feedback.** Figure 5 describes these components in one familiar technological system—an oven.

Technological systems are designed to achieve a particular **goal**, or purpose. An **input** is something that is put into a system in order to reach that goal. The **process** is a sequence of actions that the system undergoes. An **output** is a result or product. If the system works correctly, the output should match the goal. Some technological systems have an additional component, called feedback. **Feedback** is information a system uses to monitor the input, process, and output so that the system can adjust itself to meet the goal.

Go Online

SciLINKS NSTA

For: Links on technology
Visit: www.SciLinks.org
Web Code: scn-1631

Reading Checkpoint **What do all systems have in common?**

Section 1 Assessment

Target Reading Skill Previewing Visuals Refer to your questions and answers about Figure 3 to help you answer Question 2 below.

Reviewing Key Concepts

1. a. Reviewing What is technology?
   b. Applying Concepts How does a telephone fulfill the definition of technology?

2. a. Identifying Which field—science or technology—modifies the world to meet human needs or solve problems?
   b. Comparing and Contrasting How are science and technology different?
   c. Making Judgments Do you think that the development of a new, powerful telescope could be possible without a knowledge of science? How could the new telescope help advance science?

3. a. Explaining Explain why technology is always changing.

   b. Sequencing Place these technologies in the correct order: emerging technology, obsolete technology, current technology.
   c. Inferring Why do you think computer products become obsolete so quickly?

4. a. Reviewing What four components do all technological systems include? What fifth component do some systems also have?
   b. Applying Concepts An alarm clock is a technological system. Identify each component in this system.

Lab zone At-Home **Activity**

Technology Hunt With a family member, look around your home for ten examples of technology. In a table, list each item and the area of technology it represents. Describe how each item extends your abilities and how your life might be different without it.

Investigating a Technological System

Problem

How do the parts of a pen work together as a system?

Skills Focus

observing, inferring, predicting

Materials

- retractable pen
- small tray to hold the pen parts
- paper

Procedure

1. Examine the retractable pen that your teacher gives you. Predict how many parts make up the pen.

2. Disassemble the pen completely. Be careful not to break or lose any of the parts. In your notebook, draw each part and describe what function it might serve.

3. Reassemble the pen. Click the pen on and off a few times, and then write with it. As you perform these actions, think about the sequence of events taking place inside the pen. Draw one or more diagrams to explain the process that takes place.

4. Think about how the pen functions as a technological system. In your notebook, describe the goal of the pen as a system. In addition, identify the inputs, process, and outputs of the system. Does the pen system include feedback?

5. Identify any of the pen parts that might not be essential for meeting the system's goal. Then take the pen apart again and remove those parts. Reassemble the pen without them and test whether or not the pen functions.

Analyze and Conclude

1. **Observing** How many parts make up the pen system? Of those parts, how many are essential to the pen's function? What purpose do the nonessential parts serve?

2. **Inferring** What kind of input do you need to provide to make the pen work? Describe the process and output that result from the input you provide.

3. **Predicting** How might adding scent to the ink impact the sales of the pen?

4. **Forming Operational Definitions** Based on what you learned in this investigation, describe in your own words what is meant by the term *technological system*.

5. **Communicating** Suppose that you had never used or even seen a retractable pen before today. Write a letter to a friend about this remarkable device and how it works.

More to Explore

Choose another everyday device, such as a paper punch, a kitchen tool, or a child's toy. Observe the device closely to learn how it functions as a system. Then identify the system's goal, inputs, process, outputs, and feedback.

Technology Design Skills

Reading Preview

Key Concepts
- What are the steps in the technology design process, and what is involved in each step?
- What are patents?

Key Terms
- engineer
- brainstorming
- constraint
- trade-off
- prototype
- troubleshooting
- patent

Target Reading Skill

Sequencing A sequence is the order in which a series of events occurs. As you read, make a flowchart that shows the steps in the technology design process. Put the steps of the process in separate boxes in the flowchart in the order in which they typically occur.

The Technology Design Process

Identify the need.

↓

Research the problem.

↓

⌄‾⌄

Discover Activity

Why Redesign?
1. Use the materials your teacher gives you to design and construct a boat out of aluminum foil. Your goal is to make a boat that will float and carry as many pennies as possible.
2. Test your aluminum-foil boat against those of two other students to see how well your design works.
3. Based on your observations in Step 2, change the design of your boat, if necessary. Build a new boat and test it again.

Think It Over
Problem Solving What problems did you identify by testing your boat? How did you improve upon your original boat's design?

With dizzying speed, you move the cursor up, down, left, right, and all over the computer screen. Menus pop up. Folders open and close. You control the cursor with your "mouse," a device you probably don't think much about. The mouse translates the motion of your hand into direction signals the computer can read.

Have you ever wondered about the mouse's design—what it is made of and how its parts function together? The design of the mouse is the key to its success as a technology.

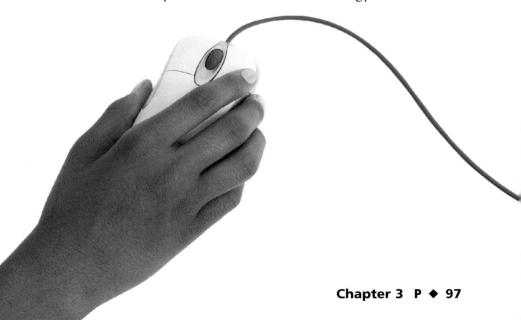

FIGURE 6
The Computer Mouse
The design of a mouse is important to its usefulness and success as a technology.

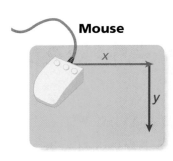

Mouse

Computer Screen

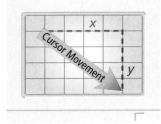

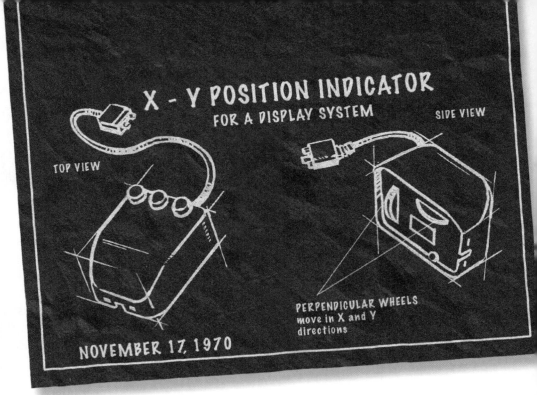

X - Y POSITION INDICATOR
FOR A DISPLAY SYSTEM

TOP VIEW

SIDE VIEW

PERPENDICULAR WHEELS
move in X and Y
directions

NOVEMBER 17, 1970

FIGURE 7
The Original Mouse
The original mouse was known as an X-Y position indicator. Moving the mouse signaled the cursor to move on the screen. Today's mouse works in a similar way.
Comparing and Contrasting *What differences do you notice between the original mouse and the ones in use today?*

Identifying a Need

The mouse was originally designed for use with large, complex computers. Early versions, such as the one in Figure 7, had several problems. For one thing, they were expensive. In addition, dirt easily became trapped in the mechanism, preventing the mouse from working. Also, the mouse often "slipped," meaning that the cursor didn't move when the mouse moved.

How did the modern mouse develop from the clunky one of the past? The modern mouse was the result of a technology design process. The technology design process is a method by which an idea for a new technology is developed into a final product. This process is sometimes called the engineering design process because it often involves the work of engineers. An **engineer** is a person who is trained to use both technological and scientific knowledge to solve practical problems.

Imagine that you are an engineer on the team that is redesigning the original mouse. What is the first thing your team should do? As your first step, you must decide exactly what need you are trying to meet. **When engineers identify a need, they clearly define the problem they are trying to solve.**

The overall need that the engineering team identified was for a reliable device that would be easy for anybody to use. In addition, the device should not cost too much and should be easy to manufacture. And, of course, the mouse must be safe, work well, and last a long time.

 **Reading Checkpoint** What problems did the early mouse have?

Researching the Problem

What is the next stage for the engineering team? **After defining a problem, engineers need to research it fully. When engineers research a problem, they gather information that will help them in their tasks.**

There are many ways that engineers obtain information related to the product they are designing. The engineers may read books and articles about the topic. They may also attend conferences, where they can share ideas with other researchers. Engineers usually perform experiments related to the technology they are designing. In addition, engineers often talk to people like you to find out what customers want.

In gathering information about the mouse, the engineers conducted many tests. They discovered that the ball inside the mouse was held in place by a complex system of sensitive, costly parts. Because the parts were so sensitive, too much pressure on the ball made it slip frequently. Any bit of dirt or dust would jam up the system. This problem caused the mouse to stop working about once a week. To fix it, the entire mouse had to be taken apart, and each part had to be cleaned separately.

Go Online
active art

For: Technology Design Process activity
Visit: PHSchool.com
Web Code: cgp-6032

FIGURE 8
The Technology Design Process

Engineers begin the technology design process by identifying a need. They then research the problem to gather information that may help them design a solution.

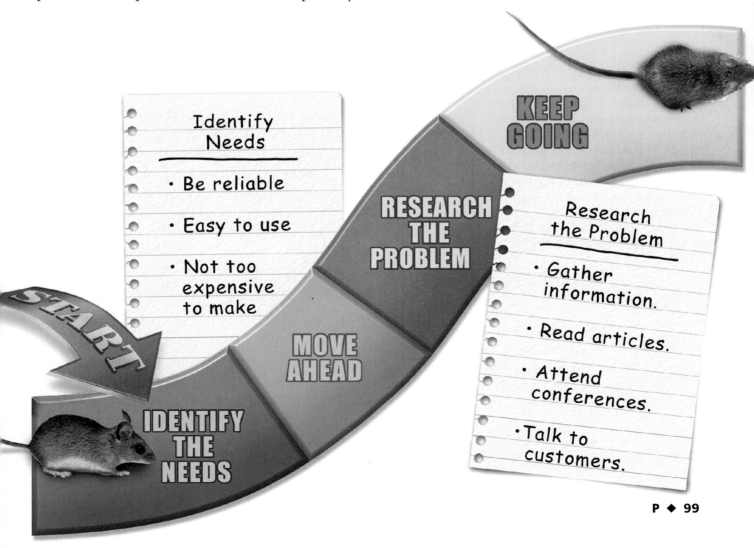

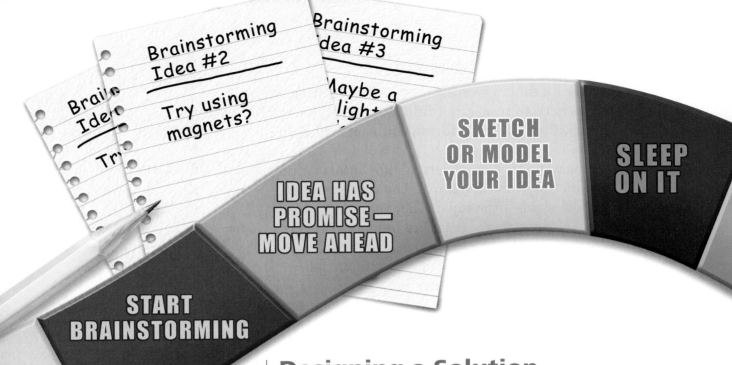

START BRAINSTORMING

IDEA HAS PROMISE— MOVE AHEAD

SKETCH OR MODEL YOUR IDEA

SLEEP ON IT

Brainstorming Idea #2

Try using magnets?

Brainstorming Idea #3

Maybe a light?

FIGURE 9
Designing a Solution
Brainstorming leads to several possible design solutions. Sketching and modeling help engineers visualize different designs. In choosing the best design, engineers must evaluate constraints and make trade-offs. Notice that engineers sometimes need to go back and repeat one or more steps.
Relating Cause and Effect Why might a design team need to rethink their ideas?

Designing a Solution

Once a team has a clear understanding of the problem, it is time to start thinking about solutions. **Designing a solution involves coming up with ideas, or thinking about different ways to solve the problem. Engineers weigh many possible solutions and choose the best one.** The best design is the one that meets the needs and has the fewest negative characteristics.

Generating Ideas An important activity that helps generate ideas is called brainstorming. **Brainstorming** is a process in which group members freely suggest any creative solutions that come to mind. Some ideas come in a flash of inspiration. When the mouse engineers brainstormed, they proposed solutions that involved magnets, lights, and other creative ideas.

After brainstorming, engineers may refine their ideas by making sketches or constructing models. The models may be three-dimensional or computer-generated. Playing with a model can spark even more ideas. Many ideas for the mouse actually came from a model an engineer built—using a butter dish and the ball from a container of roll-on deodorant!

Evaluating Constraints Can a design idea actually work? If so, how well? To answer the questions, engineers must evaluate the constraints of each possible design. A **constraint** is any factor that limits or restricts a design. For example, one physical characteristic that may affect how well a mouse functions is friction. Friction is the force created when two surfaces rub against each other. What do you suppose would happen if the ball inside the mouse were made of a smooth material with too little "grip"? It would likely slip.

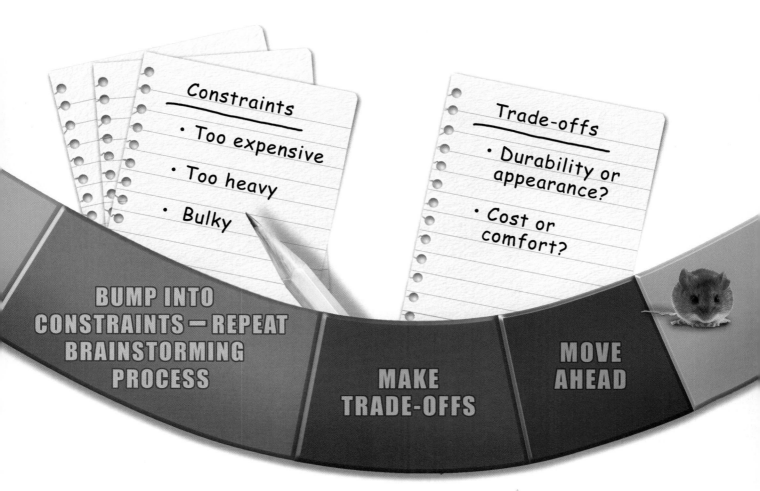

Constraints
- Too expensive
- Too heavy
- Bulky

Trade-offs
- Durability or appearance?
- Cost or comfort?

BUMP INTO CONSTRAINTS — REPEAT BRAINSTORMING PROCESS

MAKE TRADE-OFFS

MOVE AHEAD

Another physical constraint that engineers must consider is the strength of the materials they use. For example, they must think about how well the parts will stand up to repeated use. They must also consider whether the product would be likely to break and cause injuries.

Additional constraints might relate to how much money the finished product can cost and the overall size and appearance of the product. The amount of time needed to manufacture a product can be an additional constraint that engineers must consider.

Making Trade-Offs A team must sometimes make trade-offs on some features of the design. A **trade-off** is an exchange in which one benefit is given up in order to obtain another. For example, one material may be sturdy but look ugly. Another material may be more attractive but may be weaker. The design team may decide to use the more attractive material so that the product will appeal to customers. In this case, the team would be trading off strength for appearance.

 **Reading Checkpoint** What are two examples of constraints that engineers might need to consider?

Lab zone Try This Activity

Watch Ideas Take Off

In this activity, you will model some stages of the design process.

1. With a team of three or four classmates, brainstorm some ideas for a new product that would keep shoelaces from constantly untying.

2. Evaluate each idea, and discuss the constraints and trade-offs you might have to make.

3. Sketch the design solution the team has agreed on.

Predicting What do you think is the next step your team should take, after selecting a design solution?

BUILD PROTOTYPE   KEEP GOING   BEGIN TEST PHASE   END TEST PHASE

FIGURE 10
Testing a Prototype
Prototypes are built to test particular aspects of a design. This woman is testing an aircraft design in a wind tunnel. The tests will tell her how the design performs at high speeds.

Discovery
CHANNEL
SCHOOL™

Technology and Engineering

Video Preview
▶ Video Field Trip
Video Assessment

Building a Prototype

After considering constraints and trade-offs, engineers select the design with the most promise. The next phase of the process is to build and test a prototype. A **prototype** is a working model used to test a design. Many prototypes are full size and made of the materials proposed for the final product. Today, many prototypes are completely "virtual," or computer generated.

Prototypes are used to test the operation of a product, including how well it works, how long it lasts, and how safe it is to use. A team might test a prototype by having a small group of people use it and complete a questionnaire. Engineers may also test the prototype in a laboratory to see how it functions. Or they may use computers to test virtual models. The test results help determine how well the product meets the goals and what improvements are needed.

The engineers designed many tests to study the new mouse. For example, they designed a machine that kept the mouse working constantly all day. They found that after the equivalent of three years of constant use, the mouse showed only minor problems in performance.

 Reading Checkpoint **What is a virtual prototype?**

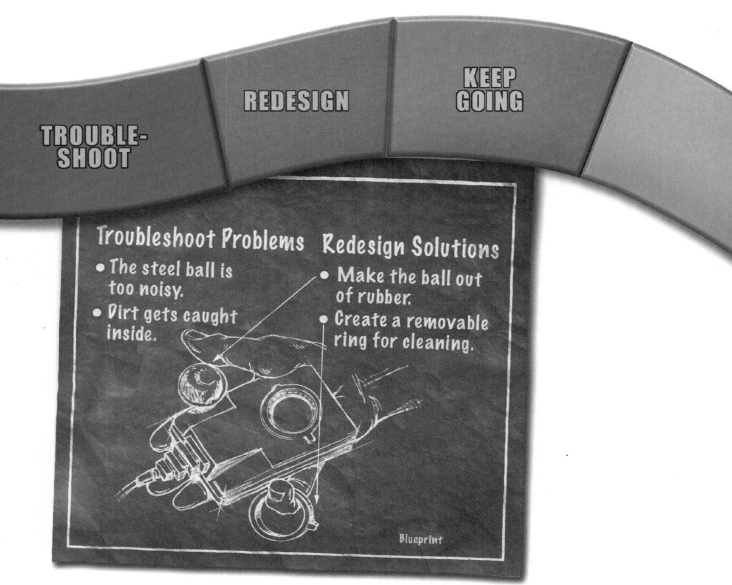

Troubleshoot Problems
- The steel ball is too noisy.
- Dirt gets caught inside.

Redesign Solutions
- Make the ball out of rubber.
- Create a removable ring for cleaning.

Blueprint

Troubleshooting and Redesigning

Prototype tests may indicate problems with the design. For example, tests may show that people have a hard time using a product or that a part breaks easily. **The next stage in the design process is to identify the causes of any problems and to redesign the product to address the problems.** The process of analyzing a design problem and finding a way to fix it is called **troubleshooting.**

Prototype tests revealed some problems with the mouse. For example, the mouse was noisy. Through troubleshooting, the engineers identified the rolling steel ball as the cause of the noise. The engineers replaced the steel ball with a rubber ball. This made the mouse quieter and less likely to slip. Engineers also added a ring-shaped cap that users could open without a tool. This redesign made the mouse easy to clean.

FIGURE 11
Troubleshooting and Redesigning
Engineers use feedback from prototype tests to troubleshoot issues and improve their design.
Making Judgments *Why is it wise to provide time and money to redesign a product?*

Reading Checkpoint **What does the process of troubleshooting involve?**

To Do

• Plan a presentation.

• Meet with marketing team.

• Talk to manufacturing group.

FIGURE 12
Communicating the Solution
Engineers must communicate information about their design solution to many groups of people. Presentations about a new technology help bring information to consumers. **Making Judgments** *What kind of information might be most important for consumers to know about a new product?*

Communicating the Solution

What happens after a design has been tested successfully? The team will want to share its accomplishments! The last stage of the technology design process is communicating the solution.

Engineers must communicate to consumers how a product meets their needs. They must also communicate with those involved in bringing the product to consumers. For example, engineers need to explain the design to manufacturers who will produce the product. The engineers must also describe their ideas to marketing people, who will advertise the product. In their presentations, engineers may use slides, models, charts, and graphs to show their ideas.

Through effective communication, information about the mouse reached the public, and the mouse became increasingly popular over the next few years. The mouse solution developed decades ago remains successful today.

 Reading Checkpoint) **What tools may an engineer use to communicate to others about a design?**

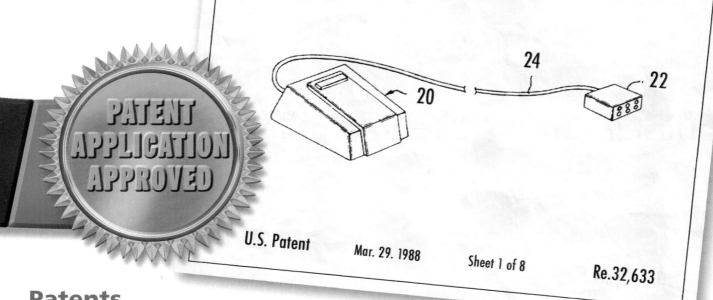

U.S. Patent   Mar. 29. 1988   Sheet 1 of 8   Re.32,633

Patents

You have seen how the engineering process can turn a good idea into a final product people can use. Because new products may bring fame or wealth to an inventor or company, **patents are usually obtained to protect the inventions. A patent is a legal document issued by a government that gives the inventor exclusive rights to make, use, or sell the invention for a limited time.** If others want to use the invention, they must obtain the patent owner's permission. After the patent's time runs out, however, anyone can make or sell the invention. An inventor may begin a patent application while the design is still in progress. Figure 13 shows part of the patent application for the mouse.

FIGURE 13
Patents
Patent applications often contain diagrams and details about a product's design. The mouse patent application included the diagram shown here.

Section 2 Assessment

Target Reading Skill Sequencing Refer to your flowchart about the technology design process as you answer Question 1.

Reviewing Key Concepts

1. a. Listing List the stages in the technology design process. Describe each stage in a sentence.
b. Explaining What are design constraints? Give two examples of constraints that should be considered when designing a cellphone.
c. Making Judgments A team working on a new bicycle seat design must choose between a comfortable but costly material and a less expensive but uncomfortable material. Which trade-off would you make? Explain.

2. a. Defining What is a patent?
b. Explaining Creativity is a key part of the design process. Explain how patents help reward creativity.
c. Inferring Why do you think patents remain in effect only for a limited time, rather than forever?

Writing in Science

How-to Paragraph Think about the computer mouse you use most frequently. Suppose your team of engineers has just finished designing this mouse model. Write clear, step-by-step instructions explaining how to use the mouse to move a cursor on a computer screen. You can include a sketch of the mouse to help clarify the instructions.

Design and Build "Egg-ceptional" Packaging

Problem

Can you design and build protective packaging for a breakable object?

Skills Focus

evaluating the design, troubleshooting

Materials

- raw eggs
- plastic bags
- meter stick
- various packaging materials provided by your teacher
- tape
- scissors
- modeling clay

Procedure

PART 1 Research and Investigate

1. Mold a piece of modeling clay into the shape of an egg.

2. Hold the clay egg 2 meters above a hard surface. Drop the egg. Examine the egg carefully for damage from the fall. Record your observations in a data table.

3. Reshape the clay egg so it looks like it did in Step 1. Then, choose one of the packaging materials and wrap it around the egg. Repeat Step 2.

4. Repeat Step 3 two more times using different packaging materials each time. Be sure to reshape the egg before each new test.

PART 2 Design and Build

5. Based on what you learned in Part 1, design protective packaging for an uncooked egg. Your packaging should
   - prevent the egg from cracking when dropped onto a hard surface from a height of 2 meters
   - use the least amount of packaging material possible
   - be made from materials that are easy to obtain

6. Sketch your design on a sheet of paper and list the materials you will use. You can use materials from Part 1, or other appropriate materials.

7. Obtain your teacher's approval of your design. Then, insert a raw egg in a plastic bag and build your protective packaging around the egg.

PART 3 Evaluate and Redesign

8. Your teacher will designate a location where you can drop the egg to test your protective packaging. After the test, unwrap the package and evaluate how well it protected the egg.

9. Based on your results, determine how you might redesign your packaging. Then, make the improvements and test the redesigned packaging with another egg.

Analyze and Conclude

1. **Designing a Solution** What did you learn from Part 1 that influenced the design of your protective package? For example, what did you learn about each of the packaging materials you tested?

2. **Evaluating the Design** Did your packaging prevent the egg from breaking? If so, which aspects of your design do you think were the most important in protecting the egg? If not, why not?

3. **Troubleshooting** How did you decide what changes to make in redesigning your packaging? How well did your redesigned packaging work to protect the egg?

4. **Working With Design Constraints** How did factors such as gravity and the fragile nature of the egg affect your design? What limits did the design criteria in Step 5 place on your packaging design?

5. **Evaluating the Impact on Society** Imagine that you work for a company that designs bicycle and skateboard helmets. How would the technology design process you used in this lab apply to the helmet company? What additional factors would you need to consider in designing helmets?

Communicate

You work in the advertising department of a company that specializes in shipping valuable and breakable antiques. Design an ad for your company that highlights your protective packaging designs.

Technology and Society

Reading Preview

Key Concepts
- How is technology tied to history?
- How does technology affect people in both positive and negative ways?
- Why is it important to analyze the risks and benefits of a technology?

Key Term
- risk-benefit analysis

Target Reading Skill
Relating Cause and Effect As you read, identify one positive and one negative effect of each technology discussed in this section. Write the information in a graphic organizer like the one below.

Effects

Cause

Invention of air bags	→	Positive effect: saves lives
	→	

Discover Activity

How Does Technology Affect Your Life?

1. Your teacher will divide the class into groups. Your group should choose a technology product that you rely on or use every day. Think about how the product affects your life.

2. List the advantages of using the product—the ways in which it helps you and improves your life.

3. Now list the disadvantages of the product.

Think It Over
Inferring Do you think that the product you chose has had an overall positive or negative impact on people? Explain.

Your hands fly across the loom. Proudly, you look at the beautiful pattern that begins to take shape in the cloth you are making. You've spent years learning the craft of weaving. Now you are skilled at it, like your father and grandfather before you.

But a factory in town is starting to use a new technology—looms run by steam power. People can operate these machines with little training. An unskilled worker can produce more cloth in a day than you can in weeks. You are about to lose your way of life.

This was the bleak prospect that weavers in England faced in the early 1800s. The new machines threatened their jobs. Some people rebelled against the idea of being replaced by machines. They invaded factories and smashed the machinery.

Hand Loom
It took about **three days** to weave the material for one shirt.

Technology's Impact on Society

The situation of the skilled weavers is one example of how technology can affect society. The term *society* refers to any group of people who live together in an area, large or small, and have certain things in common, such as a form of government. **In every age of history, technology has had a large impact on society, from the Stone Age thousands of years ago to the Information Age today.** During the Stone Age, for example, people used stones to make tools. Spears, axes, and spades enabled people to hunt animals and grow crops. As the food supply became more stable, people no longer needed to wander in search of food. They began to settle in farming communities and stay in one place.

During the Iron Age, people produced iron, a strong metal. They used iron to make weapons and tools such as chisels and saws. Many machines were also invented during the Iron Age, such as water wheels and grain mills. These inventions enabled farmers to grow more food. As food supplies increased, many people left farm life behind and moved to towns and cities.

There are many other examples from history of the huge impact that technology has had. Today, in the Information Age, cellphones, satellites, and super-fast computers allow people to share information quickly around the world. Societies in distant parts of the world are no longer really isolated from one another. The Information Age has dramatically changed the way that people live, work, and play.

✓ **Reading Checkpoint** What is a society?

FIGURE 14

Technology Through History

Before the 1800s, skilled weavers produced cloth on hand looms. In the early 1800s, steam-powered looms increased the pace of production. Today, even more powerful machines churn out cloth at high speed.

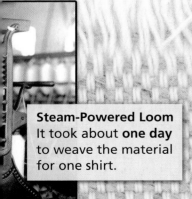

Steam-Powered Loom
It took about **one day** to weave the material for one shirt.

Modern Loom
It takes **less than a minute** to weave the material for one shirt.

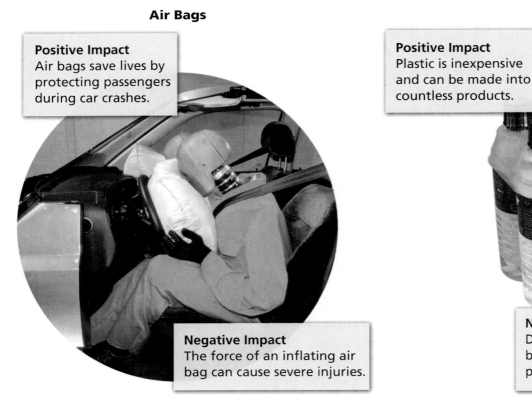

Air Bags

Positive Impact
Air bags save lives by protecting passengers during car crashes.

Negative Impact
The force of an inflating air bag can cause severe injuries.

Plastics

Positive Impact
Plastic is inexpensive and can be made into countless products.

Negative Impact
Discarded plastic products break down slowly and pollute the environment.

FIGURE 15
The Impact of Technology
Technology does not provide perfect solutions. Air bags and plastics, for example, were designed to improve the quality of life. However, they can also have negative impacts.
Inferring *Why might the negative consequences of a technology remain unrecognized for a while?*

Impacts of Technology— Good and Bad

As you can see, technological advances have done much to move societies forward through the centuries. However, it is important to keep in mind that technology has both good and bad impacts on society. **In addition to positive effects, technology can have negative consequences.** Often, many of the negative consequences are unintentional and are not recognized until long after the technology has been put to use.

Health and Safety From bandages to medicines, technology products that improve people's health and safety are all around you. These products make it possible to live longer and healthier lives. For example, air bags shown in Figure 15, have saved thousands of lives. Air bags were designed to protect people in a car crash. During a crash, air bags fill with gases and cushion passengers from the impact of the crash.

Unfortunately, however, air bags also have consequences they were never meant to have. Sometimes air bags have caused injury or even death. Small children, for example, can be severely injured by the explosive force of an inflating air bag. The hot gases that fill an air bag can also cause serious burns.

The Environment Many technologies, such as roads, dams, and pesticides affect the enviornment. For example, pesticides have played a very important role in food production. Because pesticides protect crops from insects, farmers can produce more crops and feed more people. Therefore, food prices can stay low while crop yields stay high.

However, humans and other animals can sometimes be harmed if they eat foods containing pesticides. Pesticides can also be washed by rain into rivers, streams, and water supplies. The pesticides can then affect plants and animals that live in the water, as well as the people who depend on the water supply.

Jobs Technological advances make many jobs easier to perform. They also increase the amount of work that people can accomplish. For example, farmers can plow more land faster, using a tractor than a horse-drawn plow.

However, in some cases, the advance of technology can cause people to lose their jobs. If farmers cannot afford expensive equipment, such as tractors and irrigation systems, their farms may not be as productive as farms that can. Eventually, less productive farms may go out of business and the farmers may lose their jobs. Similarly, factory and office workers may lose their jobs if machines can perform the same work more efficiently. This was the case with the weavers and other crafts people during the 1800s.

Math ▶ Analyzing Data

Working on the Farm

The graph shows the percentage of workers who worked on farms between the years 1860 and 2000. Use the graph to answer the following questions.

1. **Reading Graphs** What factor is plotted on the horizontal axis? What factor is plotted on the vertical axis?

2. **Interpreting Data** Of the years shown on the graph, in which year was the percentage of farm workers highest? In which year was the percentage lowest?

3. **Calculating** By how much did the percentage of farm workers change between 1860 and 2000?

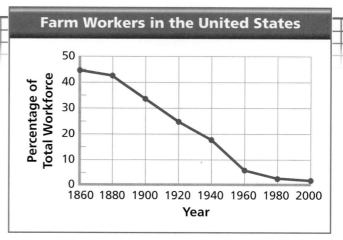

Farm Workers in the United States

4. **Drawing Conclusions** What trend does the graph show?

5. **Inferring** Based on what you know about technological advances, how would you explain the trend shown in the graph?

Pace of Life From daily chores to long-distance travel, technological advances enable people to accomplish things much more quickly today. Microwave ovens and frozen foods help you prepare meals in minutes. Planes can take you to the other side of the globe in one day. Computers, electronic equipment, and powerful machinery enable workers to accomplish more tasks in shorter time frames.

Being able to do things quickly, however, may also make people feel stressed or rushed. Life had a much slower pace only a few decades ago. People had fewer choices about where they went, what they did, or the speed at which tasks were accomplished. For example, before plane travel was available, visiting another state may have taken days. But people seldom felt as rushed as they do today, and families spent more time together.

 **Reading Checkpoint** **Why is life so fast-paced today?**

• Tech & Design in History •

Everyday Technology
There are lots of technological devices that you probably take for granted. What would your life be like if these items had not been invented?

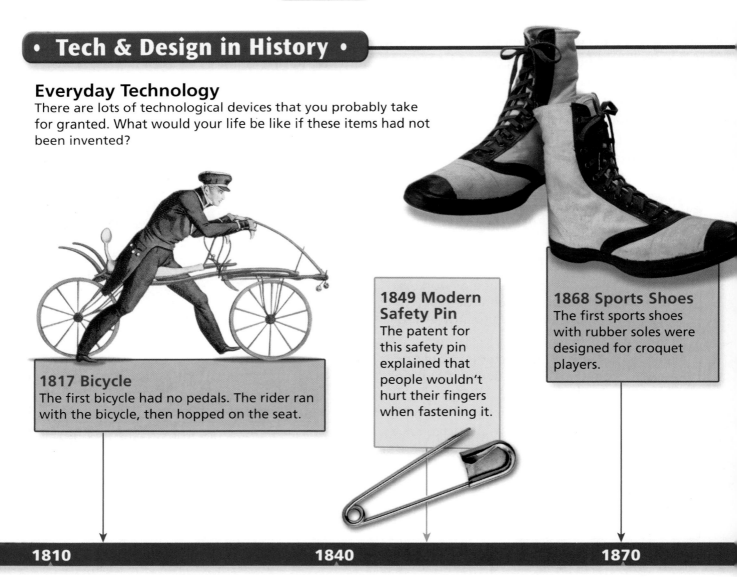

1817 Bicycle
The first bicycle had no pedals. The rider ran with the bicycle, then hopped on the seat.

1849 Modern Safety Pin
The patent for this safety pin explained that people wouldn't hurt their fingers when fastening it.

1868 Sports Shoes
The first sports shoes with rubber soles were designed for croquet players.

1810   1840   1870

Analyzing Risks and Benefits

If technology can create problems, how then can people decide whether or not to use a new technology? And how do governments determine whether a new technology should be regulated, or limited by laws?

In deciding whether to use a particular technology—or how to use it—people must analyze its possible risks and benefits. The process of **risk-benefit analysis** involves evaluating the possible problems, or risks, of a technology compared to the expected advantages, or benefits. This analysis requires logical thinking and common sense. Different people may make different decisions about whether—and how—a technology should be used.

Writing in Science

Research and Write Choose one invention described in the timeline and find out more about it. Write a short biography of the inventor and discuss the events that led up to the invention.

1891 Toothpaste Tube
Before squeezable tubes were used, toothpaste came in jars.

1904 Ice Cream Cone
At the St. Louis World's Fair, people ate ice cream in cone-shaped waffles.

1917 Zipper
This invention was the first fastening device with interlocking metal teeth. It came with an instruction booklet!

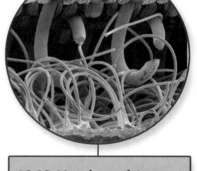

1948 Hook and Loop Fastener
The inventor of this fastener came home from a hike in the woods covered with burs. Studying the burs under the microscope, he discovered many tiny, stiff hooks—which enable the burs to cling to the soft loops in fabric!

1900   **1930**   **1960**

Identifying the Risks and Benefits Look at Figure 16 to see how risk-benefit analysis can help you make a personal decision, such as whether or not to use headphones. Risk-benefit analysis also helps governments establish regulations about new technology products. For example, suppose a company has developed a new bicycle helmet made of a lightweight material. The helmet provides less protection than older, heavier helmets, but it is much more comfortable and stylish.

In determining whether the new helmet is acceptable safety gear, a government agency first identifies both its risks and its benefits. The main risk of the new helmet is the greater possibility of injury than with heavier helmets. But because some riders find heavier helmets uncomfortable and unattractive, they may avoid wearing helmets at all. Since the new helmet is more comfortable and looks better, more people may wear it. The benefit of the new helmet, then, is that more people would have some form of head protection, rather than no protection at all.

Values and Trade-Offs Often, in evaluating a technology's risks and benefits, individuals and societies must consider human values. A value is something that a person or society regards as important, such as health, honesty, convenience, and personal freedom.

FIGURE 16
The Risks and Benefits of Using Headphones
Should you use headphones? Evaluating the risks and benefits can help you decide.
Problem Solving *What decision would you make, and why?*

Risks

- Can damage hearing at high volumes

- Can prevent you from hearing on-coming traffic, horns, and sirens

- Can be easily lost

Benefits

- Allow you to listen to your own music without disturbing others

- Can tune out loud noises and other distractions in environment

- Can be easily carried

Difficulties can arise when different values conflict—when one value favors a technology while another value cautions against it. In the case of the new helmets, the conflicting values could be safety versus people's freedom of choice. When values conflict, a decision involves trade-offs. As you learned in Section 2, a trade-off consists of exchanging one benefit for another. For example, by choosing the lightweight helmet, people trade safety for style.

Using Technology Wisely Technology will continue to play a large role in the lives of most people. That is why it is important to remember that technology does not provide perfect solutions to the problems it helps solve. Also keep in mind that technology cannot solve every problem. For example, suppose your friend dreams of being a famous singer but cannot sing. Unfortunately, even the most high-tech equipment might not help your friend sing.

It is also important to keep in mind that technology affects society as a whole. Therefore, everyone must make informed decisions to reduce the negative impacts of technology and to use technology wisely. Everyone—including you—has a role to play in determining how the technologies of today shape the world of tomorrow.

Go Online

SciLINKS NSTA

For: Links on technology and society
Visit: www.SciLinks.org
Web Code: scn-1633

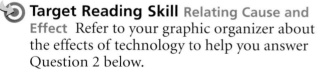

Section 3 Assessment

Target Reading Skill Relating Cause and Effect Refer to your graphic organizer about the effects of technology to help you answer Question 2 below.

Reviewing Key Concepts

1. a. **Reviewing** Give one example of how technological advances affected the society in which they were introduced.
   b. **Making Judgments** Do you think that technology has had a greater impact on society in the past or today? Explain.

2. a. **Explaining** Explain this statement: Technology does not provide perfect solutions to the problems it helps solve.
   b. **Applying Concepts** Suppose a robot that cooks meals in minutes has been invented. What positive impacts might it have?
   c. **Relating Cause and Effect** What negative impacts might the robot have over time on jobs, the pace of life, and other things?

3. a. **Defining** What is a risk-benefit analysis?
   b. **Problem Solving** What risks and benefits should be considered when deciding whether or not to buy an insect repellent?
   c. **Making Judgments** Do you think that government agencies should perform risk-benefit analyses on all insect repellents? Explain your reasoning.

Writing in Science

Summary Suppose you are a curator of a history museum. You are organizing an exhibit featuring inventions that have had dramatic impacts on society. Choose one invention that changed people's lives after it was invented. Write a summary about the invention to be posted at the exhibit.

whales | Search

The Internet

What's one quick way to find out about the latest hit movie? Or to learn why humpback whales sing? The answer is to check the Internet. The Internet links millions of computers around the globe. From your desk, you can research data, send and receive e-mails, listen to music, read the news, or just "chat."

The Information Superhighway

The Internet began in the 1960s when some government, university, and research computers were connected so that users could share data. Today, tens of millions of people use the Internet each day. Most people connect to the Internet through personal computers located at home, school, a library, or work. The data travels from one computer to another along telephone lines, wireless links, or satellites.

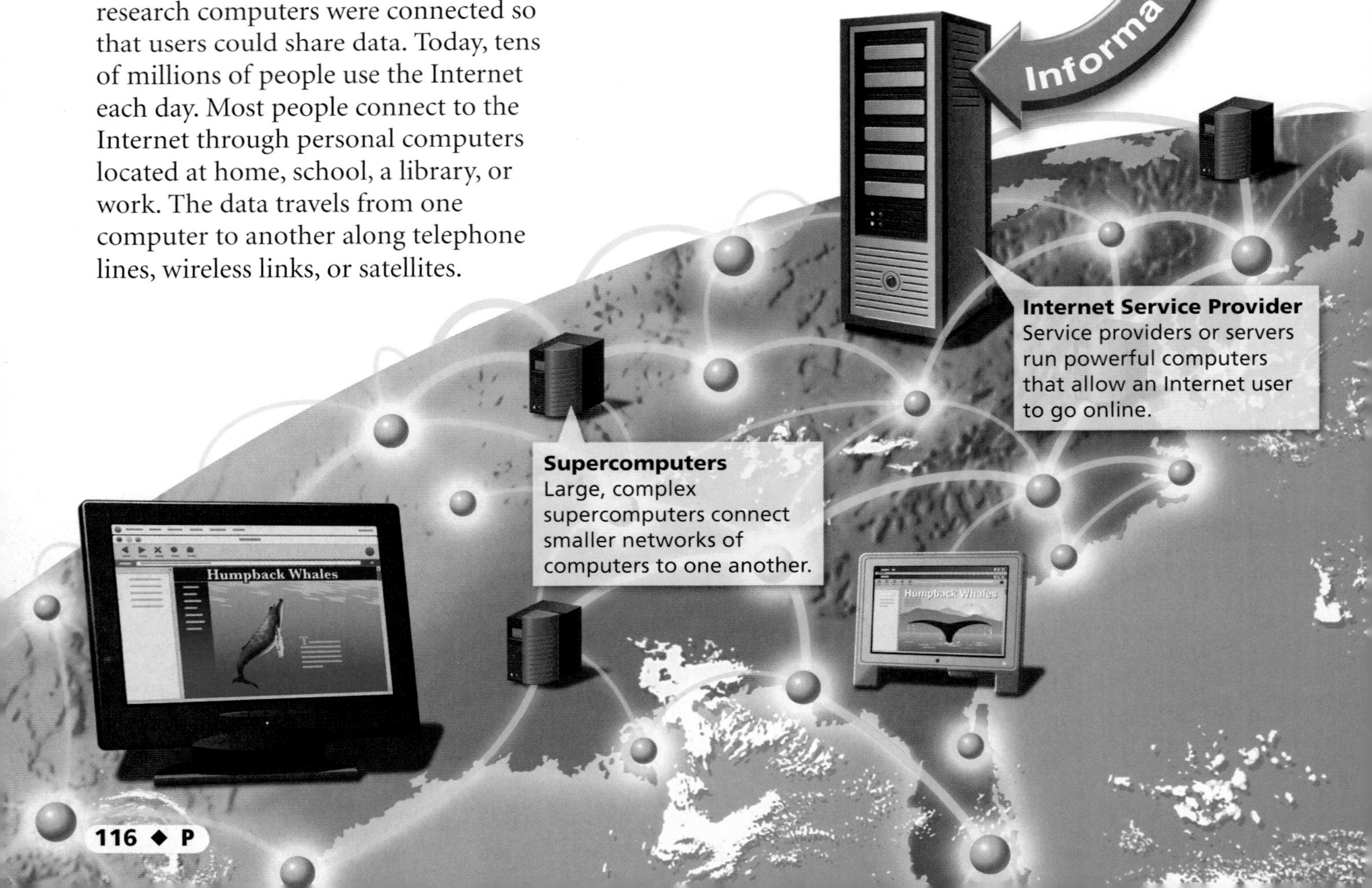

Computer and Modem
The computer stores information. The modem translates that information into a form that can be exchanged with other computers.

Information

Internet Service Provider
Service providers or servers run powerful computers that allow an Internet user to go online.

Supercomputers
Large, complex supercomputers connect smaller networks of computers to one another.

Humpback Whales

Humpback Whales

Too Much Information?

The Internet contains huge volumes of data that can be stored, accessed, and transmitted within minutes. This quick transfer of information has many benefits.

The Internet is fast, but people must consider the drawbacks. Not all the information posted on the Internet is accurate or appropriate. In addition, viruses can be transmitted via the Internet and damage the computers that receive them. Another drawback is that Internet users must own their own computer or have access to one. There is also a service fee to access the Internet.

Weigh the Impact

1. Identify the Need
Why was the Internet formed?

2. Research
Using the Internet, research the following topic—the reliability of Internet sources. List ways to evaluate the accuracy of information gathered on the Internet.

3. Write
Use what you learned to create an informative brochure on using Internet resources. Be sure to outline the steps students should take to determine the accuracy of Internet sources.

For: More on the Internet
Visit: PHSchool.com
Web Code: cgh-6030

Communications Satellite
Information travels from computers on Earth to satellites in orbit, and back to computers on Earth.

Ground Station

Ground Station

Router
Communication links connect servers and providers to other computers called routers. Routers monitor the flow of information over the Internet to determine the best route, or path, for sending data. Routers also make sure that data goes to the right destination.

Communication Links
Information travels through communication links, such as telephone lines, cable television connections, fiber-optic lines, or satellites.

① Understanding Technology

Key Concepts

- The goal of technology is to improve the way people live.

- Science is the study of the natural world to understand how it functions. Technology changes, or modifies, the natural world to meet human needs or solve problems.

- Technology progresses as people's knowledge increases and as new needs can be satisfied.

- A technological system includes a goal, inputs, processes, outputs, and, in some cases, feedback.

Key Terms

technology
obsolete
system
goal
input
process
output
feedback

② Technology Design Skills

Key Concepts

- When engineers identify a need, they clearly define the problem they are trying to solve.

- When researching a problem, engineers gather information that will help them in their tasks.

- Designing a solution involves thinking about different ways to solve the problem, and then choosing the best one.

- Prototypes are used to test the operation of a product.

- After testing a prototype, engineers identify the causes of any problems and redesign the product to address the problems.

- The last stage of the technology design process is communicating the solution.

- A patent is a legal document that gives the inventor exclusive rights to make, use, or sell the invention for a limited time.

Key Terms

engineer
brainstorming
constraint
trade-off
prototype
troubleshooting
patent

③ Technology and Society

Key Concepts

- Technology has always had a large impact on society, from the Stone Age thousands of years ago to the Information Age today.

- In addition to positive effects, technology can have negative consequences.

- In deciding whether to use a particular technology—or how to use it—people must analyze its possible risks and benefits.

Key Term

risk-benefit analysis

Review and Assessment

Go Online
PHSchool.com
For: Self-Assessment
Visit: PHSchool.com
Web Code: cga-6030

Organizing Information

Comparing and Contrasting Copy the Venn diagram comparing science and technology onto a separate sheet of paper. Then complete it and add a title. (For more on Comparing and Contrasting, see the Skills Handbook.)

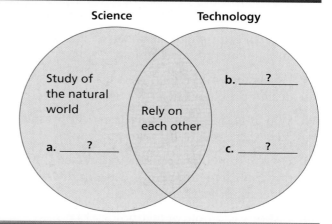

Science   Technology

Study of the natural world

a. _____?_____

Rely on each other

b. _____?_____

c. _____?_____

Reviewing Key Terms

Choose the letter of the best answer.

1. An obsolete technology is one that is
   a. currently used.
   b. high tech.
   c. broken.
   d. no longer being used.

2. The sequence of actions that a technological system undergoes is called the
   a. input.   b. feedback.
   c. process.   d. output.

3. Any factor that limits or restricts the design of a technology product is a
   a. prototype.   b. patent.
   c. trade-off.   d. constraint.

4. The process of identifying the causes of any problems in a design and finding ways to fix them is called
   a. troubleshooting.
   b. prototyping.
   c. patenting.
   d. communicating.

5. The process of evaluating the possible problems of a technology compared to its expected advantages is called
   a. feedback.
   b. risk-benefit analysis.
   c. brainstorming.
   d. prototyping.

If the statement is true, write *true*. If it is false, change the underlined word or words to make the statement true.

6. <u>Science</u> is how people change the natural world around them to meet their needs.

7. All <u>systems</u> are made of parts that work together.

8. An <u>input</u> is something put into a system.

9. A <u>trade-off</u> is an exchange in which one benefit is given up in order to obtain another.

10. The government issues a <u>prototype</u> to protect a person's invention.

Writing in Science

News Report Choose a modern day technology product, such as airplanes, with which you are familiar. Imagine that you are a news reporter covering the product's first introduction to the public. Write a 30-second informative report to be broadcast on the evening news.

Discovery CHANNEL SCHOOL™

Technology and Engineering
Video Preview
Video Field Trip
▶ Video Assessment

Review and Assessment

Checking Concepts

11. What is the overall goal of technology?

12. Give an example of an obsolete technology and an emerging technology.

13. What steps might engineers take to research a design problem fully?

14. Why is building a prototype an important part of the technology design process?

15. Do you think that technology affected the lives of people living in your great-grandparents' generation? Explain.

16. List one example of technology that has increased the pace of your life. What positive and negative impact has this technology had?

17. Why is risk-benefit analysis important in deciding whether to use a new technology?

Thinking Critically

18. **Relating Cause and Effect** How might a meteorologist who tracks hurricanes depend on satellite technology? How might satellite engineers depend on the work of scientists?

19. **Classifying** For the system shown below, identify the input, process, and output.

| Car moves forward | Driver steps on gas pedal | Gas makes engine run |

20. **Problem Solving** Your team is designing a new computer keyboard. From prototype tests, you learn that the keyboard successfully reduces hand strain, but that it breaks easily. Users also complained about the keyboard's appearance. How would you proceed?

21. **Predicting** What "Age" do you think people will be living in 100 years from now? What types of technological products will be most common then?

22. **Making Judgments** How do you think consumers can best obtain information about the risks and benefits of a technology before they purchase it?

Applying Skills

Use the table to answer Questions 23–26.

This table shows the types of trains in use in the United States in 1900 and 1960.

Number of Trains in Use in the United States, 1900 and 1960

Type	1900	1960
Steam trains	37,463	374
Electric trains	200	498
Diesel trains	0	30,240

23. **Interpreting Data** What kinds of trains existed in the United States in 1900? In 1960?

24. **Calculating** How did the number of steam trains change between 1900 and 1960? How did the number of electric and diesel trains change?

25. **Inferring** Which type of train met people's needs best in 1960? What is your evidence?

26. **Drawing Conclusions** Based on this table, what can you conclude about the progress of train technology between 1900 and 1960?

Lab zone Chapter **Project**

Performance Assessment Before testing your chair, explain to your classmates why you designed your chair the way you did. How did you join the pieces of cardboard together? How did you address the design constraints? When you test your model, examine how sturdy your chair is while supporting 20 kilograms of books. How could you improve your chair's design?

Standardized Test Prep

Choose the letter of the best answer.

1. A jacket made of a new, lightweight material has just been designed. Which of the following prototypes could be used to test how comfortable the jacket is to wear?
 A a computer model of the jacket
 B a miniature version of the jacket
 C a full-sized version of the jacket, made of cotton
 D a full-sized version of the jacket, made of the new material

2. Engineers have designed a car with a new engine and body design. Which of the following trade-offs would have a negative impact on public safety?
 F choosing lower-cost materials over good results in crash tests
 G choosing the appearance of the car seats over their comfort
 H choosing to install a more powerful music system over a better air conditioning system
 J choosing a more powerful engine over better gas mileage

3. A new robotic vacuum cleaner that was developed this year is an example of
 A an obsolete technology.
 B an emerging technology.
 C a construction technology.
 D a communication technology.

Use the graph below to answer Questions 4–5. The graph shows predicted worldwide sales of digital versatile disc (DVD) recorders.

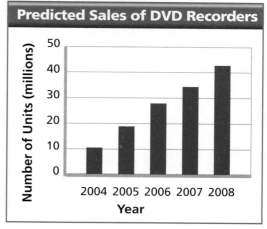

4. What are predicted sales for the year 2006?
 F 100,000   G 1,000,000
 H 280,000   J 28,000,000

5. What prediction can you make about the sale of DVD recorders after 2008?
 A No DVD recorders will be sold in 2009.
 B People will buy DVD recorders forever.
 C People will continue to buy DVD recorders until a new technology better fulfills their needs.
 D The number of DVD recorders sold will be unaffected by any emerging technology.

Constructed Response

6. Suppose a newly designed robot automatically scans products at checkout lines in supermarkets. The robot can perform no other function. The cost to install a robot at a cash register is less than the cost of hiring a cashier. Describe some of the positive and negative impacts that this new technology might have on society.

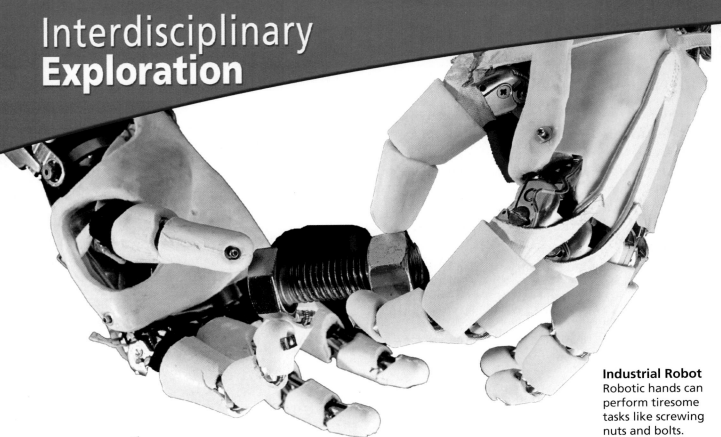

Industrial Robot
Robotic hands can perform tiresome tasks like screwing nuts and bolts.

Robots—
At Your Service

**Nanobots—
Small Robots**
Robots in the future may be even smaller than this one.

What type of machine can

* explore shipwrecks on the ocean floor?
* collect samples from distant planets?
* assemble parts with hands?
* squeeze into tight spaces?

You are probably familiar with robots in movies, television shows, and science-fiction writing. Those robots often resemble humans. They are able to talk, think, and feel. But in reality a robot is a machine with a computer. The computer is programmed or instructed to do specific tasks. For example, a robot might be programmed to pick up trash, snake through pipes, or even perform delicate surgery.

The term *robot* comes from the Czech word *robota*, meaning "forced labor" or "servant." The idea of using robots as servants is not new. But it's only in the last fifty years that scientists and engineers have developed the technology to design and build working robots. Robots have already changed our way of life. Soon, they may be everywhere.

Designing Robots

The design of a robot depends on its purpose. For example, suppose a factory that makes TVs needs the parts screwed together with tiny screws. For that task, engineers might design a robotic hand that uses a screwdriver. The energy to power the robotic hand might come from electric energy, solar energy, or batteries.

Some robots are able to gather information from the environment. These robots collect data from sensors—devices that act like eyes, ears, and skin. NASA (the National Aeronautics and Space Administration) designed Yosi (below) to explore distant planets. The robot has wires that work as touch sensors. Yosi receives and sends data to the main computer and to the people in charge. Eventually, Yosi may have a visual sensor—a camera.

Many robots are designed to move. Moving on wheels is the easiest way for a robot to travel. Wheels remain stable on the ground. Moving on two legs is the most difficult. As soon as one leg lifts off the ground, the other leg must balance and support the robot. Moving on six or eight legs, like an ant or a spider, provides more stability.

Yosi, the SpiderBot
Yosi is about 18 centimeters high and has 6 legs. Yosi's main computer controls capacitors. They build up and release stored energy from the batteries.

Antenna
Radio receiver and transmitter communicates with people in control.

Capacitor
Energy from the capacitors runs the motors.

Touch Sensor
Wires work as feelers to tell when Yosi is about to run into objects.

Motor
Motors make the legs move.

Solar Panel
Panels will collect and transform energy from the sun.

Leg and Foot
By keeping 3 legs on the ground, the other 3 legs are free to move. Feet with cleats grip the ground.

Science Activity

Work with classmates to show how a robot might collect data through touch. Follow these steps.

1. Place a large cardboard box on a desk. Tape a piece of sheer fabric over the opening of the box. Then turn the box on its side so that the fabric hangs down over the opening.

2. Place an object that cannot easily be identified inside the box—without your classmates observing you. Make sure the fabric hides the object. Then, have your partner use a wooden dowel to "feel" the object and to guess what it might be.

3. Have your partner repeat Step 2, using his or her hands instead of a dowel. How did the information gathered by using his or her hands compare to that gathered by using a dowel?

Robots Coming Your Way

How do robots affect your life? Robots may already make your life easier. Robots exist that mow lawns, vacuum houses, and give museum tours. Robots can even guard your home. And did you know that robots are used in manufacturing many products, including cars and computers?

In 1961, scientists developed the first industrial robot to work on a factory assembly line. The robot followed step-by-step instructions to weld car parts. Today, industrial robots are often faster and more efficient than humans. They don't get bored, daydream, or look at the clock! Unfortunately, some workers have lost their jobs to robots. Most job losses have occurred in the automobile industry, which uses the most robots.

Robots are expensive to make. But robots feel no pain and have no fear. Therefore, they can tackle jobs that are too difficult, dangerous, or unhealthful for humans. For example, in 1985, a robot explored the ocean floor about 4 kilometers beneath the surface and found the shipwrecked *Titanic*. In 1994, scientists sent the robot *Dante II* into a live volcano in Alaska to collect data on poisonous gases. In 1997 and 2004, NASA sent robots to Mars to take photographs and retrieve rocks and dust samples.

Dante II
In 1994, *Dante II* explored Mt. Spurr volcano in Alaska.

Oberon
In 2003, this undersea robot photographed the Great Barrier Reef off Australia.

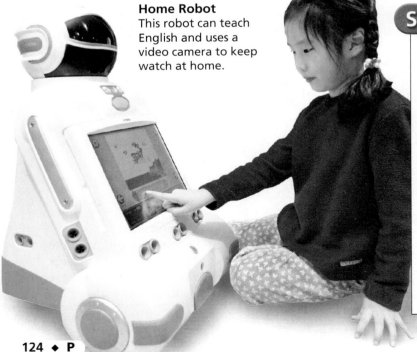

Home Robot
This robot can teach English and uses a video camera to keep watch at home.

Social Studies Activity

Robots are found in both the home and the environment. They are used in space exploration, medicine, military operations, and entertainment. Research the robots used in one of these areas. Then, make a timeline about the robots.

- Research the robots used in an industry, such as in space exploration.

- Find out when each robot was invented, what it looks like, and what its functions are.

- Make a timeline about the robots that includes dates and labels. Work with your classmates to combine your timelines. Add photos and captions.

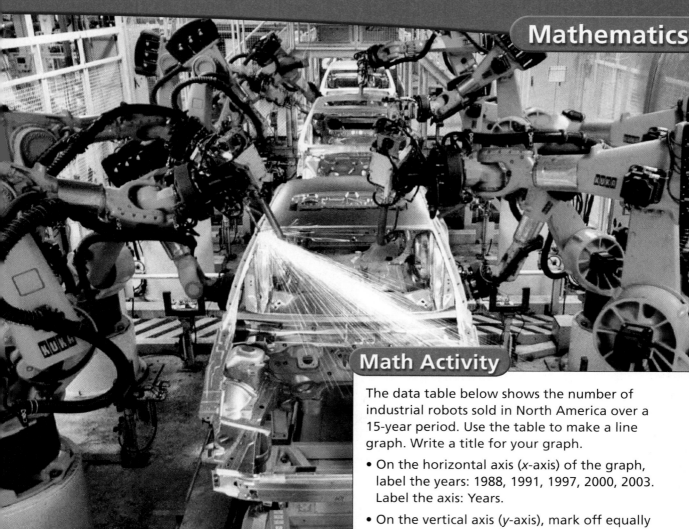

Math Activity

The data table below shows the number of industrial robots sold in North America over a 15-year period. Use the table to make a line graph. Write a title for your graph.

• On the horizontal axis (*x*-axis) of the graph, label the years: 1988, 1991, 1997, 2000, 2003. Label the axis: Years.

• On the vertical axis (*y*-axis), mark off equally spaced numbers from 0 to 15. Label this axis: Unit Sales of Robots (thousands)

• Above each year, plot the correct data. Then draw a line of best fit.

• What is the general trend in sales of industrial robots between 1988 and 2003?

Automobile Factory
In this automobile assembly line, robots accurately align and weld car frames.

Robots Working Nine-to-Five

The number of robots in industry has steadily increased since the 1960s. In factories and on assembly lines today, robots lift heavy items, load equipment, bottle beverages, weld car frames, spray paint, and stamp or inspect products. Robots can also perform complicated and delicate tasks like putting together computer products. The United States is second only to Japan in the production and sale of industrial robots.

Robot Sales to Industries in North America, 1988–2003*	
Year	Robot Sales by Units**
1988	3,600
1991	4,500
1994	7,600
1997	11,500
2000	14,500
2003	13,100

*Includes the United States, Canada, and Mexico
**Rounded to the nearest hundred

Robots in Science Fiction

Science-fiction writing describes imaginary events involving science or technology. These events often occur in the future. The characters may include robots located on distant planets. In the science-fiction short story below by Isaac Asimov, the events occur on the moon. A boy and his pet robot have just returned from exploring a deep crater.

Isaac Asimov
Writer Isaac Asimov popularized science fiction. He was also a biochemist and brought his knowledge of science to literature.

A Boy's Best Friend

Jimmy was out of his spacesuit now and washed up. You always had to wash up after coming in from outside. Even Robutt had to be sprayed, but he loved it. He stood there on all fours, his little foot-long body quivering and glowing just a tiny bit, and his small head, with no mouth, with two large glassed-in eyes, and with a bump where the brain was. He squeaked until Mr. Anderson said, "Quiet, Robutt."

Mr. Anderson was smiling. "We have something for you, Jimmy. It's at the rocket station now, but we'll have it tomorrow after all the tests are over. I thought I'd tell you now."

"From Earth, Dad?"

"A *dog* from Earth, son. A real dog. A Scotch terrier puppy. The first dog on the Moon. You won't need Robutt any more. We can't keep them both, you know, and some other boy or girl will have Robutt." He seemed to be waiting for Jimmy to say something, then he said, "You know what a dog is, Jimmy. It's the real thing. Robutt's only a mechanical imitation, a robot-mutt. That's how he got his name."

Jimmy frowned. "Robutt isn't an imitation, Dad. He's my dog."

"Not a real one, Jimmy. Robutt's just steel and wiring and a simple positronic* brain. It's not alive."

"He does everything I want him to do, Dad. He understands me. Sure, he's alive."

"No, son. Robutt is just a machine. It's just programmed to act the way it does. A dog *is* alive. You won't want Robutt after you have the dog."

"The dog will need a spacesuit, won't he?"

"Yes, of course. But it will be worth the money and he'll get used to it. And he won't need one in the City. You'll see the difference once he gets here."

Jimmy looked at Robutt, who was squeaking again, a very low, slow squeak, that seemed frightened. Jimmy held out his arms and Robutt was in them in one bound. Jimmy said, "What will the difference be between Robutt and the dog?"

Science-fiction writers use vivid details to create believable, realistic characters and settings in fantastic environments. Look back at the story for sensory details that Asimov uses to describe Robutt. Work with a classmate to write and design an advertisement for a robotic pet. Your ad should include

- sensory details that vividly describe the pet robot.

- persuasive language that will convince your readers to purchase this product.

- information about what the robot can see, do, and say.

Tie It Together

Robot Skit

Robot characters and their creators continue to fascinate audiences. George Lucas's *Star Wars* robots are a good example. With a group of classmates, write and perform a skit about scientists who are developing a robot.

- Brainstorm the time, setting, and characters in your skit. Who are the scientists? Where do they work? What type of robot will they design? What will the robot be programmed to do?

- Assign roles for classmates. Choose students to write the script, act in the skit, direct the actors, and help with the props.

- Write the skit. Keep it short and simple. Use some of the robot terms that you have learned to create realistic dialogue.

- Decide on costumes, sound effects, and props.

- Rehearse your skit and provide feedback to performers.

- Perform your robot skit for your class or for another class.

"It's hard to explain," said Mr. Anderson, "but it will be easy to see. The dog will *really* love you. Robutt is just adjusted to act as though it loves you."

"But, Dad, we don't know what's inside the dog, or what his feelings are. Maybe it's just acting, too."

Mr. Anderson frowned. "Jimmy, you'll *know* the difference when you experience the love of a living thing."

Jimmy held Robutt tightly. He was frowning, too, and the desperate look on his face meant that he wouldn't change his mind. He said, "But what's the difference how *they* act? How about how *I* feel?"

*futuristic

————*from "A Boy's Best Friend" in* Boys' Life, *by Isaac Asimov*

Think Like a Scientist

Scientists have a particular way of looking at the world, or scientific habits of mind. Whenever you ask a question and explore possible answers, you use many of the same skills that scientists do. Some of these skills are described on this page.

Observing

When you use one or more of your five senses to gather information about the world, you are **observing.** Hearing a dog bark, counting twelve green seeds, and smelling smoke are all observations. To increase the power of their senses, scientists sometimes use microscopes, telescopes, or other instruments that help them make more detailed observations.

An observation must be an accurate report of what your senses detect. It is important to keep careful records of your observations in science class by writing or drawing in a notebook. The information collected through observations is called evidence, or data.

Inferring

When you interpret an observation, you are **inferring,** or making an inference. For example, if you hear your dog barking, you may infer that someone is at your front door. To make this inference, you combine the evidence—the barking dog—and your experience or knowledge—you know that your dog barks when strangers approach—to reach a logical conclusion.

Notice that an inference is not a fact; it is only one of many possible interpretations for an observation. For example, your dog may be barking because it wants to go for a walk. An inference may turn out to be incorrect even if it is based on accurate observations and logical reasoning. The only way to find out if an inference is correct is to investigate further.

Predicting

When you listen to the weather forecast, you hear many predictions about the next day's weather—what the temperature will be, whether it will rain, and how windy it will be. Weather forecasters use observations and knowledge of weather patterns to predict the weather. The skill of **predicting** involves making an inference about a future event based on current evidence or past experience.

Because a prediction is an inference, it may prove to be false. In science class, you can test some of your predictions by doing experiments. For example, suppose you predict that larger paper airplanes can fly farther than smaller airplanes. How could you test your prediction?

Activity

Use the photograph to answer the questions below.

Observing Look closely at the photograph. List at least three observations.

Inferring Use your observations to make an inference about what has happened. What experience or knowledge did you use to make the inference?

Predicting Predict what will happen next. On what evidence or experience do you base your prediction?

Classifying

Could you imagine searching for a book in the library if the books were shelved in no particular order? Your trip to the library would be an all-day event! Luckily, librarians group together books on similar topics or by the same author. Grouping together items that are alike in some way is called **classifying.** You can classify items in many ways: by size, by shape, by use, and by other important characteristics.

Like librarians, scientists use the skill of classifying to organize information and objects. When things are sorted into groups, the relationships among them become easier to understand.

> **Activity**
>
> Classify the objects in the photograph into two groups based on any characteristic you choose. Then use another characteristic to classify the objects into three groups.

Making Models

Have you ever drawn a picture to help someone understand what you were saying? Such a drawing is one type of model. A model is a picture, diagram, computer image, or other representation of a complex object or process. **Making models** helps people understand things that they cannot observe directly.

Scientists often use models to represent things that are either very large or very small, such as the planets in the solar system, or the parts of a cell. Such models are physical models—drawings or three-dimensional structures that look like the real thing. Other models are mental models—mathematical equations or words that describe how something works.

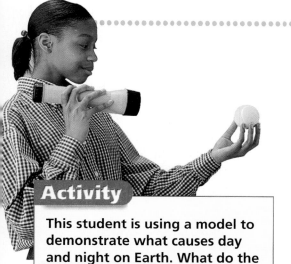

> **Activity**
>
> This student is using a model to demonstrate what causes day and night on Earth. What do the flashlight and the tennis ball in the model represent?

Communicating

Whenever you talk on the phone, write a report, or listen to your teacher at school, you are communicating. **Communicating** is the process of sharing ideas and information with other people. Communicating effectively requires many skills, including writing, reading, speaking, listening, and making models.

Scientists communicate to share results, information, and opinions. Scientists often communicate about their work in journals, over the telephone, in letters, and on the Internet.

They also attend scientific meetings where they share their ideas with one another in person.

> **Activity**
>
> On a sheet of paper, write out clear, detailed directions for tying your shoe. Then exchange directions with a partner. Follow your partner's directions exactly. How successful were you at tying your shoe? How could your partner have communicated more clearly?

Making Measurements

By measuring, scientists can express their observations more precisely and communicate more information about what they observe.

Measuring in SI

The standard system of measurement used by scientists around the world is known as the International System of Units, which is abbreviated as SI (**Système International d'Unités,** in French). SI units are easy to use because they are based on multiples of 10. Each unit is ten times larger than the next smallest unit and one tenth the size of the next largest unit. The table lists the prefixes used to name the most common SI units.

Length To measure length, or the distance between two points, the unit of measure is the **meter (m).** The distance from the floor to a doorknob is approximately one meter. Long distances, such as the distance between two cities, are measured in kilometers (km). Small lengths are measured in centimeters (cm) or millimeters (mm). Scientists use metric rulers and meter sticks to measure length.

Common SI Prefixes		
Prefix	**Symbol**	**Meaning**
kilo-	k	1,000
hecto-	h	100
deka-	da	10
deci-	d	0.1 (one tenth)
centi-	c	0.01 (one hundredth)
milli-	m	0.001 (one thousandth)

Common Conversions		
1 km	=	1,000 m
1 m	=	100 cm
1 m	=	1,000 mm
1 cm	=	10 mm

Liquid Volume To measure the volume of a liquid, or the amount of space it takes up, you will use a unit of measure known as the **liter (L).** One liter is the approximate volume of a medium-size carton of milk. Smaller volumes are measured in milliliters (mL). Scientists use graduated cylinders to measure liquid volume.

Activity

The larger lines on the metric ruler in the picture show centimeter divisions, while the smaller, unnumbered lines show millimeter divisions. How many centimeters long is the shell? How many millimeters long is it?

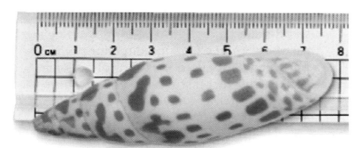

Activity

The graduated cylinder in the picture is marked in milliliter divisions. Notice that the water in the cylinder has a curved surface. This curved surface is called the *meniscus.* To measure the volume, you must read the level at the lowest point of the meniscus. What is the volume of water in this graduated cylinder?

Common Conversion
1 L = 1,000 mL

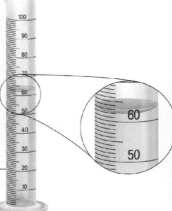

Mass To measure mass, or the amount of matter in an object, you will use a unit of measure known as the **gram (g).** One gram is approximately the mass of a paper clip. Larger masses are measured in kilograms (kg). Scientists use a balance to find the mass of an object.

Common Conversion

1 kg = 1,000 g

Activity

The mass of the potato in the picture is measured in kilograms. What is the mass of the potato? Suppose a recipe for potato salad called for one kilogram of potatoes. About how many potatoes would you need?

0.25 KG

Temperature To measure the temperature of a substance, you will use the **Celsius scale.** Temperature is measured in degrees Celsius (°C) using a Celsius thermometer. Water freezes at 0°C and boils at 100°C.

Time The unit scientists use to measure time is the **second (s).**

Activity

What is the temperature of the liquid in degrees Celsius?

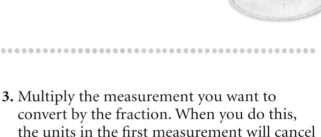

Converting SI Units

To use the SI system, you must know how to convert between units. Converting from one unit to another involves the skill of **calculating,** or using mathematical operations. Converting between SI units is similar to converting between dollars and dimes because both systems are based on multiples of ten.

Suppose you want to convert a length of 80 centimeters to meters. Follow these steps to convert between units.

1. Begin by writing down the measurement you want to convert—in this example, 80 centimeters.

2. Write a conversion factor that represents the relationship between the two units you are converting. In this example, the relationship is 1 meter = 100 centimeters. Write this conversion factor as a fraction, making sure to place the units you are converting from (centimeters, in this example) in the denominator.

3. Multiply the measurement you want to convert by the fraction. When you do this, the units in the first measurement will cancel out with the units in the denominator. Your answer will be in the units you are converting to (meters, in this example).

Example

80 centimeters = ■ meters

$$80 \text{ centimeters} \times \frac{1 \text{ meter}}{100 \text{ centimeters}} = \frac{80 \text{ meters}}{100}$$
$$= 0.8 \text{ meters}$$

Activity

Convert between the following units.
1. 600 millimeters = ■ meters
2. 0.35 liters = ■ milliliters
3. 1,050 grams = ■ kilograms

Conducting a Scientific Investigation

In some ways, scientists are like detectives, piecing together clues to learn about a process or event. One way that scientists gather clues is by carrying out experiments. An experiment tests an idea in a careful, orderly manner. Although experiments do not all follow the same steps in the same order, many follow a pattern similar to the one described here.

Posing Questions

Experiments begin by asking a scientific question. A scientific question is one that can be answered by gathering evidence. For example, the question "Which freezes faster—fresh water or salt water?" is a scientific question because you can carry out an investigation and gather information to answer the question.

Developing a Hypothesis

The next step is to form a hypothesis. A **hypothesis** is a possible explanation for a set of observations or answer to a scientific question. In science, a hypothesis must be something that can be tested. A hypothesis can be worded as an *If . . . then . . .* statement. For example, a hypothesis might be *"If I add salt to fresh water, then the water will take longer to freeze."* A hypothesis worded this way serves as a rough outline of the experiment you should perform.

Designing an Experiment

Next you need to plan a way to test your hypothesis. Your plan should be written out as a step-by-step procedure and should describe the observations or measurements you will make.

Two important steps involved in designing an experiment are controlling variables and forming operational definitions.

Controlling Variables In a well-designed experiment, you need to keep all variables the same except for one. A **variable** is any factor that can change in an experiment. The factor that you change is called the **manipulated variable**. In this experiment, the manipulated variable is the amount of salt added to the water. Other factors, such as the amount of water or the starting temperature, are kept constant.

The factor that changes as a result of the manipulated variable is called the **responding variable.** The responding variable is what you measure or observe to obtain your results. In this experiment, the responding variable is how long the water takes to freeze.

An experiment in which all factors except one are kept constant is called a **controlled experiment.** Most controlled experiments include a test called the control. In this experiment, Container 3 is the control. Because no salt is added to Container 3, you can compare the results from the other containers to it. Any difference in results must be due to the addition of salt alone.

Forming Operational Definitions Another important aspect of a well-designed experiment is having clear operational definitions. An **operational definition** is a statement that describes how a particular variable is to be measured or how a term is to be defined. For example, in this experiment, how will you determine if the water has frozen? You might decide to insert a stick in each container at the start of the experiment. Your operational definition of "frozen" would be the time at which the stick can no longer move.

Experimental Procedure
1. Fill 3 containers with 300 milliliters of cold tap water.
2. Add 10 grams of salt to Container 1; stir. Add 20 grams of salt to Container 2; stir. Add no salt to Container 3.
3. Place the 3 containers in a freezer.
4. Check the containers every 15 minutes. Record your observations.

Interpreting Data

The observations and measurements you make in an experiment are called **data.** At the end of an experiment, you need to analyze the data to look for any patterns or trends. Patterns often become clear if you organize your data in a data table or graph. Then think through what the data reveal. Do they support your hypothesis? Do they point out a flaw in your experiment? Do you need to collect more data?

Drawing Conclusions

A **conclusion** is a statement that sums up what you have learned from an experiment. When you draw a conclusion, you need to decide whether the data you collected support your hypothesis or not. You may need to repeat an experiment several times before you can draw any conclusions from it. Conclusions often lead you to pose new questions and plan new experiments to answer them.

Activity

Is a ball's bounce affected by the height from which it is dropped? Using the steps just described, plan a controlled experiment to investigate this problem.

Technology Design Skills

Engineers are people who use scientific and technological knowledge to solve practical problems. To design new products, engineers usually follow the process described here, even though they may not follow these steps in the exact order. As you read the steps, think about how you might apply them in technology labs.

Identify a Need

Before engineers begin designing a new product, they must first identify the need they are trying to meet. For example, suppose you are a member of a design team in a company that makes toys. Your team has identified a need: a toy boat that is inexpensive and easy to assemble.

Research the Problem

Engineers often begin by gathering information that will help them with their new design. This research may include finding articles in books, magazines, or on the Internet. It may also include talking to other engineers who have solved similar problems. Engineers often perform experiments related to the product they want to design.

For your toy boat, you could look at toys that are similar to the one you want to design. You might do research on the Internet. You could also test some materials to see whether they will work well in a toy boat.

Drawing for a boat design ▼

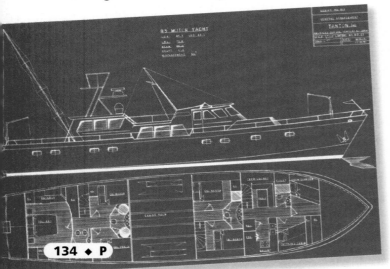

134 ◆ P

Design a Solution

Research gives engineers information that helps them design a product. When engineers design new products, they usually work in teams.

Generating Ideas Often design teams hold brainstorming meetings in which any team member can contribute ideas. **Brainstorming** is a creative process in which one team member's suggestions often spark ideas in other group members. Brainstorming can lead to new approaches to solving a design problem.

Evaluating Constraints During brainstorming, a design team will often come up with several possible designs. The team must then evaluate each one.

As part of their evaluation, engineers consider constraints. **Constraints** are factors that limit or restrict a product design. Physical characteristics, such as the properties of materials used to make your toy boat, are constraints. Money and time are also constraints. If the materials in a product cost a lot, or if the product takes a long time to make, the design may be impractical.

Making Trade-offs Design teams usually need to make trade-offs. In a **trade-off,** engineers give up one benefit of a proposed design in order to obtain another. In designing your toy boat, you will have to make trade-offs. For example, suppose one material is sturdy but not fully waterproof. Another material is more waterproof, but breakable. You may decide to give up the benefit of sturdiness in order to obtain the benefit of waterproofing.

Build and Evaluate a Prototype

Once the team has chosen a design plan, the engineers build a prototype of the product. A **prototype** is a working model used to test a design. Engineers evaluate the prototype to see whether it works well, is easy to operate, is safe to use, and holds up to repeated use.

Think of your toy boat. What would the prototype be like? Of what materials would it be made? How would you test it?

Troubleshoot and Redesign

Few prototypes work perfectly, which is why they need to be tested. Once a design team has tested a prototype, the members analyze the results and identify any problems. The team then tries to **troubleshoot,** or fix the design problems. For example, if your toy boat leaks or wobbles, the boat should be redesigned to eliminate those problems.

Communicate the Solution

A team needs to communicate the final design to the people who will manufacture and use the product. To do this, teams may use sketches, detailed drawings, computer simulations, and word descriptions.

Activity

You can use the technology design process to design and build a toy boat.

Research and Investigate

1. Visit the library or go online to research toy boats.

2. Investigate how a toy boat can be powered, including wind, rubber bands, or baking soda and vinegar.

3. Brainstorm materials, shapes, and steering for your boat.

Design and Build

4. Based on your research, design a toy boat that
   • is made of readily available materials
   • is no larger than 15 cm long and 10 cm wide
   • includes a power system, a rudder, and an area for cargo
   • travels 2 meters in a straight line carrying a load of 100 pennies

5. Sketch your design and write a step-by-step plan for building your boat. After your teacher approves your plan, build your boat.

Evaluate and Redesign

6. Test your boat, evaluate the results, and troubleshoot any problems.

7. Based on your evaluation, redesign your toy boat so it performs better.

Creating Data Tables and Graphs

How can you make sense of the data in a science experiment?
The first step is to organize the data to help you understand them.
Data tables and graphs are helpful tools for organizing data.

Data Tables

You have gathered your materials and set up your experiment. But before you start, you need to plan a way to record what happens during the experiment. By creating a data table, you can record your observations and measurements in an orderly way.

Suppose, for example, that a scientist conducted an experiment to find out how many Calories people of different body masses burn while doing various activities. The data table shows the results.

Notice in this data table that the manipulated variable (body mass) is the heading of one column. The responding variable (for

Calories Burned in 30 Minutes			
Body Mass	Experiment 1: Bicycling	Experiment 2: Playing Basketball	Experiment 3: Watching Television
30 kg	60 Calories	120 Calories	21 Calories
40 kg	77 Calories	164 Calories	27 Calories
50 kg	95 Calories	206 Calories	33 Calories
60 kg	114 Calories	248 Calories	38 Calories

Experiment 1, the number of Calories burned while bicycling) is the heading of the next column. Additional columns were added for related experiments.

Bar Graphs

To compare how many Calories a person burns doing various activities, you could create a bar graph. A bar graph is used to display data in a number of separate, or distinct, categories. In this example, bicycling, playing basketball, and watching television are the three categories.

To create a bar graph, follow these steps.

1. On graph paper, draw a horizontal, or *x*-, axis and a vertical, or *y*-, axis.

2. Write the names of the categories to be graphed along the horizontal axis. Include an overall label for the axis as well.

3. Label the vertical axis with the name of the responding variable. Include units of measurement. Then create a scale along the axis by marking off equally spaced numbers that cover the range of the data collected.

4. For each category, draw a solid bar using the scale on the vertical axis to determine the height. Make all the bars the same width.

5. Add a title that describes the graph.

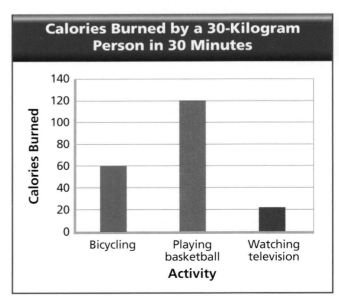

Calories Burned by a 30-Kilogram Person in 30 Minutes

Line Graphs

To see whether a relationship exists between body mass and the number of Calories burned while bicycling, you could create a line graph. A line graph is used to display data that show how one variable (the responding variable) changes in response to another variable (the manipulated variable). You can use a line graph when your manipulated variable is **continuous,** that is, when there are other points between the ones that you tested. In this example, body mass is a continuous variable because there are other body masses between 30 and 40 kilograms (for example, 31 kilograms). Time is another example of a continuous variable.

Line graphs are powerful tools because they allow you to estimate values for conditions that you did not test in the experiment. For example, you can use the line graph to estimate that a 35-kilogram person would burn 68 Calories while bicycling.

To create a line graph, follow these steps.

1. On graph paper, draw a horizontal, or *x*-, axis and a vertical, or *y*-, axis.

2. Label the horizontal axis with the name of the manipulated variable. Label the vertical axis with the name of the responding variable. Include units of measurement.

3. Create a scale on each axis by marking off equally spaced numbers that cover the range of the data collected.

4. Plot a point on the graph for each piece of data. In the line graph above, the dotted lines show how to plot the first data point (30 kilograms and 60 Calories). Follow an imaginary vertical line extending up from the horizontal axis at the 30-kilogram mark. Then follow an imaginary horizontal line extending across from the vertical axis at the 60-Calorie mark. Plot the point where the two lines intersect.

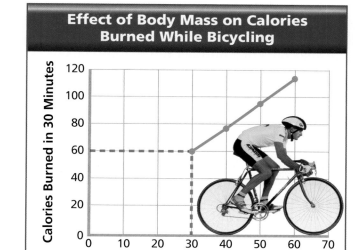

Effect of Body Mass on Calories Burned While Bicycling

5. Connect the plotted points with a solid line. (In some cases, it may be more appropriate to draw a line that shows the general trend of the plotted points. In those cases, some of the points may fall above or below the line. Also, not all graphs are linear. It may be more appropriate to draw a curve to connect the points.)

6. Add a title that identifies the variables or relationship in the graph.

Activity

Create line graphs to display the data from Experiment 2 and Experiment 3 in the data table.

Activity

You read in the newspaper that a total of 4 centimeters of rain fell in your area in June, 2.5 centimeters fell in July, and 1.5 centimeters fell in August. What type of graph would you use to display these data? Use graph paper to create the graph.

Circle Graphs

Like bar graphs, circle graphs can be used to display data in a number of separate categories. Unlike bar graphs, however, circle graphs can only be used when you have data for *all* the categories that make up a given topic. A circle graph is sometimes called a pie chart. The pie represents the entire topic, while the slices represent the individual categories. The size of a slice indicates what percentage of the whole a particular category makes up.

The data table below shows the results of a survey in which 24 teenagers were asked to identify their favorite sport. The data were then used to create the circle graph at the right.

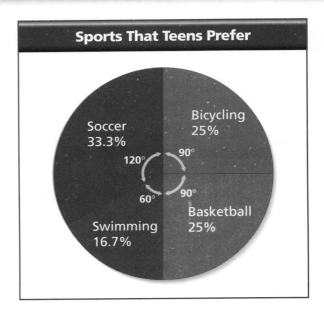

Favorite Sports	
Sport	Students
Soccer	8
Basketball	6
Bicycling	6
Swimming	4

To create a circle graph, follow these steps.

1. Use a compass to draw a circle. Mark the center with a point. Then draw a line from the center point to the top of the circle.

2. Determine the size of each "slice" by setting up a proportion where x equals the number of degrees in a slice. (*Note:* A circle contains 360 degrees.) For example, to find the number of degrees in the "soccer" slice, set up the following proportion:

$$\frac{\text{Students who prefer soccer}}{\text{Total number of students}} = \frac{x}{\text{Total number of degrees in a circle}}$$

$$\frac{8}{24} = \frac{x}{360}$$

Cross-multiply and solve for x.

$$24x = 8 \times 360$$
$$x = 120$$

The "soccer" slice should contain 120 degrees.

3. Use a protractor to measure the angle of the first slice, using the line you drew to the top of the circle as the 0° line. Draw a line from the center of the circle to the edge for the angle you measured.

4. Continue around the circle by measuring the size of each slice with the protractor. Start measuring from the edge of the previous slice so the wedges do not overlap. When you are done, the entire circle should be filled in.

5. Determine the percentage of the whole circle that each slice represents. To do this, divide the number of degrees in a slice by the total number of degrees in a circle (360), and multiply by 100%. For the "soccer" slice, you can find the percentage as follows:

$$\frac{120}{360} \times 100\% = 33.3\%$$

6. Use a different color for each slice. Label each slice with the category and with the percentage of the whole it represents.

7. Add a title to the circle graph.

Activity

In a class of 28 students, 12 students take the bus to school, 10 students walk, and 6 students ride their bicycles. Create a circle graph to display these data.

Math Review

Scientists use math to organize, analyze, and present data. This appendix will help you review some basic math skills.

Mean, Median, and Mode

The **mean** is the average, or the sum of the data divided by the number of data items. The middle number in a set of ordered data is called the **median**. The **mode** is the number that appears most often in a set of data.

Example

A scientist counted the number of distinct songs sung by seven different male birds and collected the data shown below.

Male Bird Songs							
Bird	A	B	C	D	E	F	G
Number of Songs	36	29	40	35	28	36	27

To determine the mean number of songs, add the total number of songs and divide by the number of data items—in this case, the number of male birds.

$$\text{Mean} = \frac{231}{7} = 33 \text{ songs}$$

To find the median number of songs, arrange the data in numerical order and find the number in the middle of the series.

27 28 29 35 36 36 40

The number in the middle is 35, so the median number of songs is 35.

The mode is the value that appears most frequently. In the data, 36 appears twice, while each other item appears only once. Therefore, 36 songs is the mode.

Practice

Find out how many minutes it takes each student in your class to get to school. Then find the mean, median, and mode for the data.

Probability

Probability is the chance that an event will occur. Probability can be expressed as a ratio, a fraction, or a percentage. For example, when you flip a coin, the probability that the coin will land heads up is 1 in 2, or $\frac{1}{2}$, or 50 percent.

The probability that an event will happen can be expressed in the following formula.

$$P(\text{event}) = \frac{\text{Number of times the event can occur}}{\text{Total number of possible events}}$$

Example

A paper bag contains 25 blue marbles, 5 green marbles, 5 orange marbles, and 15 yellow marbles. If you close your eyes and pick a marble from the bag, what is the probability that it will be yellow?

$$P(\text{yellow marbles}) = \frac{15 \text{ yellow marbles}}{50 \text{ marbles total}}$$

$$P = \frac{15}{50}, \text{ or } \frac{3}{10}, \text{ or } 30\%$$

Practice

Each side of a cube has a letter on it. Two sides have *A*, three sides have *B*, and one side has *C*. If you roll the cube, what is the probability that *A* will land on top?

Area

The **area** of a surface is the number of square units that cover it. The front cover of your textbook has an area of about 600 cm².

Area of a Rectangle and a Square To find the area of a rectangle, multiply its length times its width. The formula for the area of a rectangle is

$$A = \ell \times w, \text{ or } A = \ell w$$

Since all four sides of a square have the same length, the area of a square is the length of one side multiplied by itself, or squared.

$$A = s \times s, \text{ or } A = s^2$$

Example

A scientist is studying the plants in a field that measures 75 m × 45 m. What is the area of the field?

$$A = \ell \times w$$
$$A = 75 \text{ m} \times 45 \text{ m}$$
$$A = 3{,}375 \text{ m}^2$$

Area of a Circle The formula for the area of a circle is

$$A = \pi \times r \times r, \text{ or } A = \pi r^2$$

The length of the radius is represented by r, and the value of π is approximately $\frac{22}{7}$.

Example

Find the area of a circle with a radius of 14 cm.

$$A = \pi r^2$$
$$A = 14 \times 14 \times \frac{22}{7}$$
$$A = 616 \text{ cm}^2$$

Practice

Find the area of a circle that has a radius of 21 m.

Circumference

The distance around a circle is called the circumference. The formula for finding the circumference of a circle is

$$C = 2 \times \pi \times r, \text{ or } C = 2\pi r$$

Example

The radius of a circle is 35 cm. What is its circumference?

$$C = 2\pi r$$
$$C = 2 \times 35 \times \frac{22}{7}$$
$$C = 220 \text{ cm}$$

Practice

What is the circumference of a circle with a radius of 28 m?

Volume

The volume of an object is the number of cubic units it contains. The volume of a wastebasket, for example, might be about 26,000 cm³.

Volume of a Rectangular Object To find the volume of a rectangular object, multiply the object's length times its width times its height.

$$V = \ell \times w \times h, \text{ or } V = \ell w h$$

Example

Find the volume of a box with length 24 cm, width 12 cm, and height 9 cm.

$$V = \ell w h$$
$$V = 24 \text{ cm} \times 12 \text{ cm} \times 9 \text{ cm}$$
$$V = 2{,}592 \text{ cm}^3$$

Practice

What is the volume of a rectangular object with length 17 cm, width 11 cm, and height 6 cm?

Fractions

A **fraction** is a way to express a part of a whole. In the fraction $\frac{4}{7}$, 4 is the numerator and 7 is the denominator.

Adding and Subtracting Fractions To add or subtract two or more fractions that have a common denominator, first add or subtract the numerators. Then write the sum or difference over the common denominator.

To find the sum or difference of fractions with different denominators, first find the least common multiple of the denominators. This is known as the least common denominator. Then convert each fraction to equivalent fractions with the least common denominator. Add or subtract the numerators. Then write the sum or difference over the common denominator.

Example

$$\frac{5}{6} - \frac{3}{4} = \frac{10}{12} - \frac{9}{12} = \frac{10 - 9}{12} = \frac{1}{12}$$

Multiplying Fractions To multiply two fractions, first multiply the two numerators, then multiply the two denominators.

Example

$$\frac{5}{6} \times \frac{2}{3} = \frac{5 \times 2}{6 \times 3} = \frac{10}{18} = \frac{5}{9}$$

Dividing Fractions Dividing by a fraction is the same as multiplying by its reciprocal. Reciprocals are numbers whose numerators and denominators have been switched. To divide one fraction by another, first invert the fraction you are dividing by—in other words, turn it upside down. Then multiply the two fractions.

Example

$$\frac{2}{5} \div \frac{7}{8} = \frac{2}{5} \times \frac{8}{7} = \frac{2 \times 8}{5 \times 7} = \frac{16}{35}$$

Practice

Solve the following: $\frac{3}{7} \div \frac{4}{5}$.

Decimals

Fractions whose denominators are 10, 100, or some other power of 10 are often expressed as decimals. For example, the fraction $\frac{9}{10}$ can be expressed as the decimal 0.9, and the fraction $\frac{7}{100}$ can be written as 0.07.

Adding and Subtracting With Decimals To add or subtract decimals, line up the decimal points before you carry out the operation.

Example

```
   27.4          278.635
 + 6.19        − 191.4
  33.59          87.235
```

Multiplying With Decimals When you multiply two numbers with decimals, the number of decimal places in the product is equal to the total number of decimal places in each number being multiplied.

Example

```
    46.2  (one decimal place)
  × 2.37  (two decimal places)
 109.494  (three decimal places)
```

Dividing With Decimals To divide a decimal by a whole number, put the decimal point in the quotient above the decimal point in the dividend.

Example

$$15.5 \div 5$$

```
    3.1
 5)15.5
```

To divide a decimal by a decimal, you need to rewrite the divisor as a whole number. Do this by multiplying both the divisor and dividend by the same multiple of 10.

Example

$$1.68 \div 4.2 = 16.8 \div 42$$

```
    0.4
 42)16.8
```

Practice

Multiply 6.21 by 8.5.

Ratio and Proportion

A **ratio** compares two numbers by division. For example, suppose a scientist counts 800 wolves and 1,200 moose on an island. The ratio of wolves to moose can be written as a fraction, $\frac{800}{1,200}$, which can be reduced to $\frac{2}{3}$. The same ratio can also be expressed as 2 to 3 or 2 : 3.

A **proportion** is a mathematical sentence saying that two ratios are equivalent. For example, a proportion could state that $\frac{800 \text{ wolves}}{1,200 \text{ moose}} = \frac{2 \text{ wolves}}{3 \text{ moose}}$. You can sometimes set up a proportion to determine or estimate an unknown quantity. For example, suppose a scientist counts 25 beetles in an area of 10 square meters. The scientist wants to estimate the number of beetles in 100 square meters.

Example

1. Express the relationship between beetles and area as a ratio: $\frac{25}{10}$, simplified to $\frac{5}{2}$.
2. Set up a proportion, with x representing the number of beetles. The proportion can be stated as $\frac{5}{2} = \frac{x}{100}$.
3. Begin by cross-multiplying. In other words, multiply each fraction's numerator by the other fraction's denominator.

   5 × 100 = 2 × x, or 500 = 2x

4. To find the value of x, divide both sides by 2. The result is 250, or 250 beetles in 100 square meters.

Practice

Find the value of x in the following proportion: $\frac{6}{7} = \frac{x}{49}$.

Percentage

A **percentage** is a ratio that compares a number to 100. For example, there are 37 granite rocks in a collection that consists of 100 rocks. The ratio $\frac{37}{100}$ can be written as 37%. Granite rocks make up 37% of the rock collection.

You can calculate percentages of numbers other than 100 by setting up a proportion.

Example

Rain falls on 9 days out of 30 in June. What percentage of the days in June were rainy?

$$\frac{9 \text{ days}}{30 \text{ days}} = \frac{d\%}{100\%}$$

To find the value of d, begin by cross-multiplying, as for any proportion:

9 × 100 = 30 × d $d = \frac{900}{30}$ $d = 30$

Practice

There are 300 marbles in a jar, and 42 of those marbles are blue. What percentage of the marbles is blue?

Significant Figures

The **precision** of a measurement depends on the instrument you use to take the measurement. For example, if the smallest unit on the ruler is millimeters, then the most precise measurement you can make will be in millimeters.

The sum or difference of measurements can only be as precise as the least precise measurement being added or subtracted. Round your answer so that it has the same number of digits after the decimal as the least precise measurement. Round up if the last digit is 5 or more, and round down if the last digit is 4 or less.

Example

Subtract a temperature of 5.2°C from the temperature 75.46°C.

75.46 − 5.2 = 70.26

5.2 has the fewest digits after the decimal, so it is the least precise measurement. Since the last digit of the answer is 6, round up to 3. The most precise difference between the measurements is 70.3°C.

Practice

Add 26.4 m to 8.37 m. Round your answer according to the precision of the measurements.

Significant figures are the number of nonzero digits in a measurement. Zeroes between nonzero digits are also significant. For example, the measurements 12,500 L, 0.125 cm, and 2.05 kg all have three significant figures. When you multiply and divide measurements, the one with the fewest significant figures determines the number of significant figures in your answer.

Example

Multiply 110 g by 5.75 g.

110 × 5.75 = 632.5

Because 110 has only two significant figures, round the answer to 630 g.

Scientific Notation

A **factor** is a number that divides into another number with no remainder. In the example, the number 3 is used as a factor four times.

An **exponent** tells how many times a number is used as a factor. For example, $3 \times 3 \times 3 \times 3$ can be written as 3^4. The exponent 4 indicates that the number 3 is used as a factor four times. Another way of expressing this is to say that 81 is equal to 3 to the fourth power.

Example

$3^4 = 3 \times 3 \times 3 \times 3 = 81$

Scientific notation uses exponents and powers of ten to write very large or very small numbers in shorter form. When you write a number in scientific notation, you write the number as two factors. The first factor is any number between 1 and 10. The second factor is a power of 10, such as 10^3 or 10^6.

Example

The average distance between the planet Mercury and the sun is 58,000,000 km. To write the first factor in scientific notation, insert a decimal point in the original number so that you have a number between 1 and 10. In the case of 58,000,000, the number is 5.8.

To determine the power of 10, count the number of places that the decimal point moved. In this case, it moved 7 places.

58,000,000 km = 5.8 × 10^7 km

Practice

Express 6,590,000 in scientific notation.

Reading Comprehension Skills

Your textbook is an important source of science information. As you read your science textbook, you will find that the book has been written to assist you in understanding the science concepts.

Learning From Science Textbooks

As you study science in school, you will learn science concepts in a variety of ways. Sometimes you will do interesting activities and experiments to explore science ideas. To fully understand what you observe in experiments and activities, you will need to read your science textbook. To help you read, some of the important ideas are highlighted so that you can easily recognize what they are. In addition, a target reading skill in each section will help you understand what you read.

By using the target reading skills, you will improve your reading comprehension—that is, you will improve your ability to understand what you read. As you learn science, you will build knowledge that will help you understand even more of what you read. This knowledge will help you learn about all the topics presented in this textbook.

And—guess what?—these reading skills can be useful whenever you are reading. Reading to learn is important for your entire life. You have an opportunity to begin that process now.

The target reading skills that will improve your reading comprehension are described below.

Building Vocabulary

To understand the science concepts taught in this textbook, you need to remember the meanings of the Key Terms. One strategy consists of writing the definitions of these terms in your own words. You can also practice using the terms in sentences and make lists of words or phrases you associate with each term.

Using Prior Knowledge

Your prior knowledge is what you already know before you begin to read about a topic. Building on what you already know gives you a head start on learning new information. Before you begin a new assignment, think about what you know. You might page through your reading assignment, looking at the headings and the visuals to spark your memory. You can list what you know in the graphic organizer provided in the section opener. Then, as you read, consider questions like the ones below to connect what you learn to what you already know.

- How does what you learn relate to what you know?
- How did something you already know help you learn something new?
- Did your original ideas agree with what you have just learned? If not, how would you revise your original ideas?

Asking Questions

Asking yourself questions is an excellent way to focus on and remember new information in your textbook. You can learn how to ask good questions.

One way is to turn the text headings into questions. Then your questions can guide you to identify and remember the important information as you read. Look at these examples:

Heading: Using Seismographic Data

Question: How are seismographic data used?

Heading: Kinds of Faults

Question: What are the kinds of faults?

You do not have to limit your questions to the text headings. Ask questions about anything that you need to clarify or that will help you understand the content. *What* and *how* are probably the most common question words, but you may also ask *why, who, when,* or *where* questions. Here is an example:

Properties of Waves

Question	Answer
What is amplitude?	Amplitude is . . .

Previewing Visuals

Visuals are photographs, graphs, tables, diagrams, and illustrations. Visuals, such as this diagram of a normal fault, contain important information. Look at visuals and their captions before you read. This will help you prepare for what you will be reading about.

Often you will be asked what you want to learn about a visual. For example, after you look at the normal fault diagram, you might ask: What is the movement along a normal fault? Questions about visuals give you a purpose for reading—to answer your questions. Previewing visuals also helps you see what you already know.

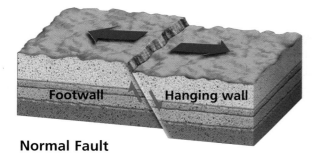

Footwall   **Hanging wall**

Normal Fault

Outlining

An outline shows the relationship between main ideas and supporting ideas. An outline has a formal structure. You write the main ideas, called topics, next to Roman numerals. The supporting ideas, sometimes called subtopics, are written under the main ideas and labeled A, B, C, and so on. An outline looks like this:

Technology and Society

I. Technology through history
II. The impact of technology on society
   A.
   B.

When you have completed an outline like this, you can see at a glance the structure of the section. You can use this outline as a study tool.

Identifying Main Ideas

When you are reading, it is important to try to understand the ideas and concepts that are in a passage. As you read science material, you will recognize that each paragraph has a lot of information and detail. Good readers try to identify the most important—or biggest—idea in every paragraph or section. That's the main idea. The other information in the paragraph supports or further explains the main idea.

Sometimes main ideas are stated directly. In this book, some main ideas are identified for you as key concepts. These are printed in bold-face type. However, you must identify other main ideas yourself. In order to do this, you must identify all the ideas within a paragraph or section. Then ask yourself which idea is big enough to include all the other ideas.

Comparing and Contrasting

When you compare and contrast, you examine the similarities and differences between things. You can compare and contrast in a Venn diagram or in a table. Your completed diagram or table shows you how the items are alike and how they are different.

Venn Diagram A Venn diagram consists of two overlapping circles. In the space where the circles overlap, you write the characteristics that the two items have in common. In one of the circles outside the area of overlap, you write the differing features or characteristics of one of the items. In the other circle outside the area of overlap, you write the differing characteristics of the other item.

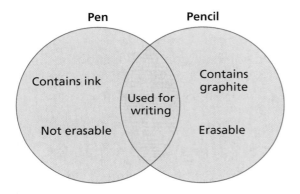

Pen / Pencil

Contains ink
Not erasable
Used for writing
Contains graphite
Erasable

Table In a compare/contrast table, you list the items to be compared across the top of the table. Then list the characteristics or features to be compared in the left column. Complete the table by filling in information about each characteristic or feature.

Blood Vessel	Function	Structure of Wall
Artery	Carries blood away from heart	
Capillary		
Vein		

Sequencing

A sequence is the order in which a series of events occurs. Recognizing and remembering the sequence of events is important to understanding many processes in science. Sometimes the text uses words like *first, next, during,* and *after* to signal a sequence. A flowchart or a cycle diagram can help you visualize a sequence.

Flowchart To make a flowchart, write a brief description of each step or event in a box. Place the boxes in order, with the first event at the top of the page. Then draw an arrow to connect each step or event to the next.

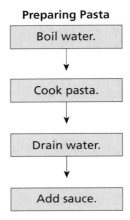

Preparing Pasta

Boil water.
↓
Cook pasta.
↓
Drain water.
↓
Add sauce.

Cycle Diagram A cycle diagram shows a sequence that is continuous, or cyclical. A continuous sequence does not have an end because when the final event is over, the first event begins again. To create a cycle diagram, write the starting event in a box placed at the top of a page in the center. Then, moving in a clockwise direction around an imaginary circle, write each event in a box in its proper sequence. Draw arrows that connect each event to the one that occurs next, forming a continuous circle.

Identifying Supporting Evidence

A hypothesis is a possible explanation for observations made by scientists or an answer to a scientific question. A hypothesis is tested over and over again. The tests may produce evidence that supports the hypothesis. When enough supporting evidence is collected, a hypothesis may become a theory.

Identifying the supporting evidence for a hypothesis or theory can help you understand the hypothesis or theory. Evidence consists of facts—information whose accuracy can be confirmed by testing or observation.

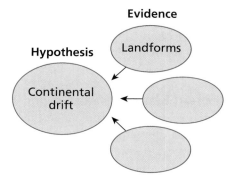

Relating Cause and Effect

Identifying causes and effects helps you understand relationships among events. A cause makes something happen. An effect is what happens. When you recognize that one event causes another, you are relating cause and effect. Words like *cause, because, effect, affect,* and *result* often signal a cause or an effect.

Sometimes an effect can have more than one cause, or a cause can produce several effects. For example, car exhaust and smoke from industrial plants are two causes of air pollution. Some effects of air pollution include breathing difficulties for some people, death of plants along some highways, and damage to some building surfaces.

Science involves many cause-and-effect relationships. Seeing and understanding these relationships helps you understand science processes.

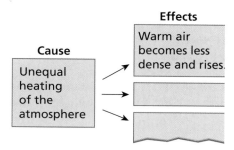

Concept Mapping

Concept maps are useful tools for organizing information on any topic. A concept map begins with a main idea or core concept and shows how the idea can be subdivided into related subconcepts or smaller ideas. In this way, relationships between concepts become clearer and easier to understand.

You construct a concept map by placing concepts (usually nouns) in ovals and connecting them with linking words. The biggest concept or idea is placed in an oval at the top of the map. Related concepts are arranged in ovals below the big idea. The linking words are often verbs and verb phrases and are written on the lines that connect the ovals.

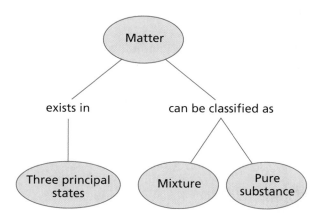

Safety Symbols

These symbols warn of possible dangers in the laboratory and remind you to work carefully.

 Safety Goggles Wear safety goggles to protect your eyes in any activity involving chemicals, flames or heating, or glassware.

 Lab Apron Wear a laboratory apron to protect your skin and clothing from damage.

 Breakage Handle breakable materials, such as glassware, with care. Do not touch broken glassware.

 Heat-Resistant Gloves Use an oven mitt or other hand protection when handling hot materials such as hot plates or hot glassware.

 Plastic Gloves Wear disposable plastic gloves when working with harmful chemicals and organisms. Keep your hands away from your face, and dispose of the gloves according to your teacher's instructions.

 Heating Use a clamp or tongs to pick up hot glassware. Do not touch hot objects with your bare hands.

 Flames Before you work with flames, tie back loose hair and clothing. Follow instructions from your teacher about lighting and extinguishing flames.

 No Flames When using flammable materials, make sure there are no flames, sparks, or other exposed heat sources present.

 Corrosive Chemical Avoid getting acid or other corrosive chemicals on your skin or clothing or in your eyes. Do not inhale the vapors. Wash your hands after the activity.

 Poison Do not let any poisonous chemical come into contact with your skin, and do not inhale its vapors. Wash your hands when you are finished with the activity.

 Fumes Work in a ventilated area when harmful vapors may be involved. Avoid inhaling vapors directly. Only test an odor when directed to do so by your teacher, and use a wafting motion to direct the vapor toward your nose.

 Sharp Object Scissors, scalpels, knives, needles, pins, and tacks can cut your skin. Always direct a sharp edge or point away from yourself and others.

 Animal Safety Treat live or preserved animals or animal parts with care to avoid harming the animals or yourself. Wash your hands when you are finished with the activity.

 Plant Safety Handle plants only as directed by your teacher. If you are allergic to certain plants, tell your teacher; do not do an activity involving those plants. Avoid touching harmful plants such as poison ivy. Wash your hands when you are finished with the activity.

 Electric Shock To avoid electric shock, never use electrical equipment around water, or when the equipment is wet or your hands are wet. Be sure cords are untangled and cannot trip anyone. Unplug equipment not in use.

 Physical Safety When an experiment involves physical activity, avoid injuring yourself or others. Alert your teacher if there is any reason you should not participate.

 Disposal Dispose of chemicals and other laboratory materials safely. Follow the instructions from your teacher.

 Hand Washing Wash your hands thoroughly when finished with the activity. Use antibacterial soap and warm water. Rinse well.

 General Safety Awareness When this symbol appears, follow the instructions provided. When you are asked to develop your own procedure in a lab, have your teacher approve your plan before you go further.

Science Safety Rules

General Precautions
Follow all instructions. Never perform activities without the approval and supervision of your teacher. Do not engage in horseplay. Never eat or drink in the laboratory. Keep work areas clean and uncluttered.

Dress Code
Wear safety goggles whenever you work with chemicals, glassware, heat sources such as burners, or any substance that might get into your eyes. If you wear contact lenses, notify your teacher.

Wear a lab apron or coat whenever you work with corrosive chemicals or substances that can stain. Wear disposable plastic gloves when working with organisms and harmful chemicals. Tie back long hair. Remove or tie back any article of clothing or jewelry that can hang down and touch chemicals, flames, or equipment. Roll up long sleeves. Never wear open shoes or sandals.

First Aid
Report all accidents, injuries, or fires to your teacher, no matter how minor. Be aware of the location of the first-aid kit, emergency equipment such as the fire extinguisher and fire blanket, and the nearest telephone. Know whom to contact in an emergency.

Heating and Fire Safety
Keep all combustible materials away from flames. When heating a substance in a test tube, make sure that the mouth of the tube is not pointed at you or anyone else. Never heat a liquid in a closed container. Use an oven mitt to pick up a container that has been heated.

Using Chemicals Safely
Never put your face near the mouth of a container that holds chemicals. Never touch, taste, or smell a chemical unless your teacher tells you to.

Use only those chemicals needed in the activity. Keep all containers closed when chemicals are not being used. Pour all chemicals over the sink or a container, not over your work surface. Dispose of excess chemicals as instructed by your teacher.

Be extra careful when working with acids or bases. When mixing an acid and water, always pour the water into the container first and then add the acid to the water. Never pour water into an acid. Wash chemical spills and splashes immediately with plenty of water.

Using Glassware Safely
If glassware is broken or chipped, notify your teacher immediately. Never handle broken or chipped glass with your bare hands.

Never force glass tubing or thermometers into a rubber stopper or rubber tubing. Have your teacher insert the glass tubing or thermometer if required for an activity.

Using Sharp Instruments
Handle sharp instruments with extreme care. Never cut material toward you; cut away from you.

Animal and Plant Safety
Never perform experiments that cause pain, discomfort, or harm to animals. Only handle animals if absolutely necessary. If you know that you are allergic to certain plants, molds, or animals, tell your teacher before doing an activity in which these are used. Wash your hands thoroughly after any activity involving animals, animal parts, plants, plant parts, or soil.

During field work, wear long pants, long sleeves, socks, and closed shoes. Avoid poisonous plants and fungi as well as plants with thorns.

End-of-Experiment Rules
Unplug all electrical equipment. Clean up your work area. Dispose of waste materials as instructed by your teacher. Wash your hands after every experiment.

The microscope is an essential tool in the study of life science. It allows you to see things that are too small to be seen with the unaided eye.

You will probably use a compound microscope like the one you see here. The compound microscope has more than one lens that magnifies the object you view.

Typically, a compound microscope has one lens in the eyepiece, the part you look through. The eyepiece lens usually magnifies 10 ×. Any object you view through this lens would appear 10 times larger than it is.

The compound microscope may contain one or two other lenses called objective lenses. If there are two objective lenses, they are called the low-power and high-power objective lenses. The low-power objective lens usually magnifies 10 ×. The high-power objective lens usually magnifies 40 ×.

To calculate the total magnification with which you are viewing an object, multiply the magnification of the eyepiece lens by the magnification of the objective lens you are using. For example, the eyepiece's magnification of 10 × multiplied by the low-power objective's magnification of 10 × equals a total magnification of 100 ×.

Use the photo of the compound microscope to become familiar with the parts of the microscope and their functions.

The Parts of a Compound Microscope

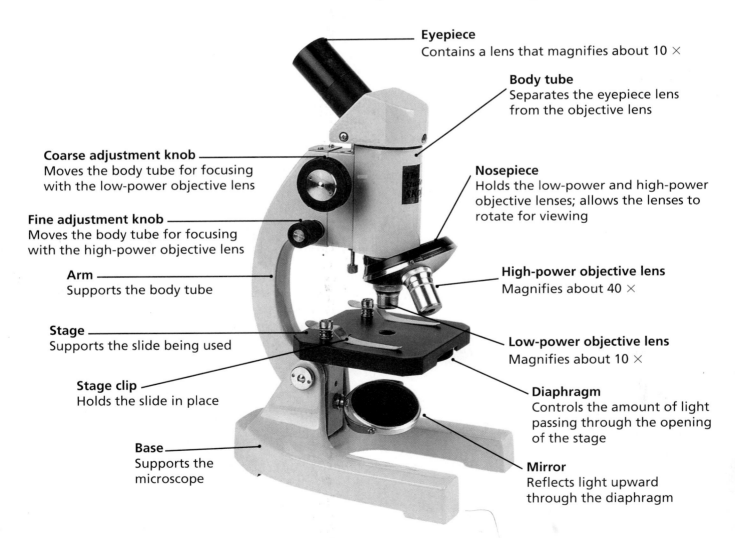

Eyepiece
Contains a lens that magnifies about 10 ×

Body tube
Separates the eyepiece lens from the objective lens

Coarse adjustment knob
Moves the body tube for focusing with the low-power objective lens

Nosepiece
Holds the low-power and high-power objective lenses; allows the lenses to rotate for viewing

Fine adjustment knob
Moves the body tube for focusing with the high-power objective lens

Arm
Supports the body tube

High-power objective lens
Magnifies about 40 ×

Stage
Supports the slide being used

Low-power objective lens
Magnifies about 10 ×

Stage clip
Holds the slide in place

Diaphragm
Controls the amount of light passing through the opening of the stage

Base
Supports the microscope

Mirror
Reflects light upward through the diaphragm

Using the Microscope

Use the following procedures when you are working with a microscope.

1. To carry the microscope, grasp the microscope's arm with one hand. Place your other hand under the base.
2. Place the microscope on a table with the arm toward you.
3. Turn the coarse adjustment knob to raise the body tube.
4. Revolve the nosepiece until the low-power objective lens clicks into place.
5. Adjust the diaphragm. While looking through the eyepiece, also adjust the mirror until you see a bright white circle of light. **CAUTION:** *Never use direct sunlight as a light source.*
6. Place a slide on the stage. Center the specimen over the opening on the stage. Use the stage clips to hold the slide in place. **CAUTION:** *Glass slides are fragile.*
7. Look at the stage from the side. Carefully turn the coarse adjustment knob to lower the body tube until the low-power objective almost touches the slide.
8. Looking through the eyepiece, very slowly turn the coarse adjustment knob until the specimen comes into focus.
9. To switch to the high-power objective lens, look at the microscope from the side. Carefully revolve the nosepiece until the high-power objective lens clicks into place. Make sure the lens does not hit the slide.
10. Looking through the eyepiece, turn the fine adjustment knob until the specimen comes into focus.

Making a Wet-Mount Slide

Use the following procedures to make a wet-mount slide of a specimen.

1. Obtain a clean microscope slide and a coverslip. **CAUTION:** *Glass slides and coverslips are fragile.*
2. Place the specimen on the slide. The specimen must be thin enough for light to pass through it.
3. Using a plastic dropper, place a drop of water on the specimen.
4. Gently place one edge of the coverslip against the slide so that it touches the edge of the water drop at a 45° angle. Slowly lower the coverslip over the specimen. If air bubbles are trapped beneath the coverslip, tap the coverslip gently with the eraser end of a pencil.
5. Remove any excess water at the edge of the coverslip with a paper towel.

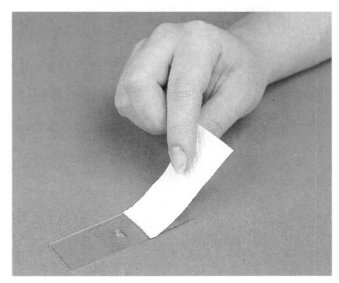

The laboratory balance is an important tool in scientific investigations. You can use a balance to determine the masses of materials that you study or experiment with in the laboratory.

Different kinds of balances are used in the laboratory. One kind of balance is the triple-beam balance. The balance that you may use in your science class is probably similar to the balance illustrated in this Appendix. To use the balance properly, you should learn the name, location, and function of each part of the balance you are using. What kind of balance do you have in your science class?

The Triple-Beam Balance

The triple-beam balance is a single-pan balance with three beams calibrated in grams. The back, or 100-gram, beam is divided into ten units of 10 grams each. The middle, or 500-gram, beam is divided into five units of 100 grams each. The front, or 10-gram, beam is divided into ten major units of 1 gram each. Each of these units is further divided into units of 0.1 gram. What is the largest mass you could find with a triple-beam balance?

The following procedure can be used to find the mass of an object with a triple-beam balance:

1. Place the object on the pan.
2. Move the rider on the middle beam notch by notch until the horizontal pointer drops below zero. Move the rider back one notch.
3. Move the rider on the back beam notch by notch until the pointer again drops below zero. Move the rider back one notch.
4. Slowly slide the rider along the front beam until the pointer stops at the zero point.
5. The mass of the object is equal to the sum of the readings on the three beams.

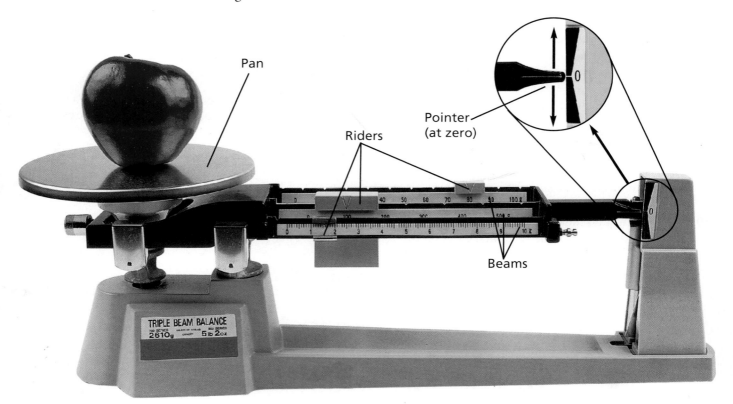

Triple-Beam Balance

A

accuracy How close a measurement is to the true or accepted value. (p. 62)
exactitud Cuán cerca está una medida del valor verdadero o aceptado.

B

brainstorming A process in which group members freely suggest any creative solutions that come to mind. (p. 100)
lluvia de ideas Proceso mediante el cual los miembros de un grupo sugieren libremente cualquier solución creativa que se les ocurre.

C

classifying The process of grouping together items that are alike in some way. (p. 10)
clasificar Proceso de agrupar objetos con algún tipo de semejanza.

communicating The process of sharing ideas with others through writing and speaking. (p. 21)
comunicar Proceso de compartir ideas con otras personas a través de la escritura o el lenguage hablado.

constraint Any factor that limits or restricts a design. (p. 100)
restricción Cualquier factor que limita o restringe un diseño.

controlled experiment An experiment in which only one variable is manipulated at a time. (p. 17)
experimento controlado Experimento en el cual sólo una variable es manipulada a la vez.

coordinate A pair of numbers used to determine the position of a point on a graph. (p. 70)
coordenada Par de números que se usa para determinar la posición de un punto en una gráfica.

D

data Facts, figures, and other evidence gathered through observations. (p. 18)
dato Hechos, cifras u otra evidencia reunida por medio de las observaciones.

data point A point on a graph showing the location of a piece of data. (p. 70)
punto de dato Punto en una gráfica que muestra la ubicación de parte de los datos.

density A measure of how much mass is contained in a given volume. (p. 52)
densidad Medida de cuánta masa contiene un determinado volumen.

E

engineer A person who is trained to use both technological and scientific knowledge to solve practical problems. (p. 98)
ingeniero Persona capacitada para usar conocimientos tecnológicos y científicos para resolver problemas prácticos.

estimate An approximation of a number based on reasonable assumptions. (p. 61)
estimación Aproximación de un número basado en conjeturas razonables.

F

feedback The information a technological system uses to monitor the input, process, and output so that the system can adjust itself to meet the goal. (p. 95)
retroalimentación Información que usa un sistema tecnológico para comprobar la entrada, proceso y salida para autoajustarse con el fin de conseguir un objetivo.

English and Spanish Glossary

G

goal The overall purpose of a technological system. (p. 95)
objetivo El propósito general de un sistema tecnológico.

graph A picture of information from a data table; shows the relationship between variables. (p. 69)
gráfica Ilustración con información de una de tabla datos; muestra la relación entre las variables.

H

horizontal axis (or x-axis) A line that runs left to right along the bottom of a graph, on which the manipulated variable (or independent variable) is labeled. (p. 70)
eje horizontal (o eje x) Recta que va de izquierda a derecha en la base de una gráfica, en la cual se rotula la variable manipulada (o variable independiente).

hypothesis A possible explanation for a set of observations or answer to a scientific question; must be testable. (p. 15)
hipótesis Explicación posible a un conjunto de observaciones o respuesta a una pregunta científica; debe ser verificable.

I

inferring The process of making an inference, an interpretation based on observations and prior knowledge. (p. 8)
inferir Proceso de realizar una inferencia; interpretación basada en observaciones y en el conocimiento previo.

input Something that is put into a technological system in order to achieve a goal. (p. 95)
entrada Algo que se agrega a un sistema tecnológico para conseguir un propósito.

L

linear graph A line graph in which the data points yield a straight line. (p. 70)
gráfica lineal Gráfica en la cual los puntos de los datos forman una línea recta.

line of best fit A smooth line that reflects the general pattern in a graph. (p. 70)
recta de mayor aproximación Recta que refleja el patrón general en una gráfica.

M

making models The process of creating representations of complex objects or processes. (p. 11)
hacer modelos Proceso de crear representaciones de objetos o procesos complejos.

manipulated variable The one factor that a scientist changes during an experiment; also called independent variable. (p. 16)
variable manipulada Único factor que un científico cambia durante un experimento; también llamada variable independiente.

mass A measure of the amount of matter an object contains. (p. 48)
masa Medida de la cantidad de materia que contiene un objeto.

mean The numerical average of the numbers in a list. (p. 66)
media Promedio numérico de los números en una lista.

median The middle number in a list of numbers. (p. 66)
mediana Número en la mitad, en una lista de números.

meniscus The curved upper surface of a liquid in a column of liquid. (p. 50)
menisco Superficie superior curvada de un líquido en una columna de líquido.

metric system A system of measurement based on the number 10. (p. 45)
sistema métrico Sistema de medida basado en el número 10.

mode The number that appears most often in a list of numbers. (p. 67)
moda Número que aparece más a menudo en una lista de números.

nonlinear graph A line graph in which the data points do not fall along a straight line. (p. 74)
gráfica no lineal Gráfica lineal en la que los puntos de datos no forman una línea recta.

observing The process of using one or more of your senses to gather information. (p. 7)
observar Proceso de usar uno o más de tus sentidos para reunir información.

obsolete No longer in use. (p. 92)
obsoleto Que ya no está en uso.

operational definition A statement that describes how to measure a particular variable or how to define a particular term. (p. 17)
definición operativa Enunciado que describe cómo medir una variable determinada o cómo definir un término determinado.

origin The point where the *x*-axis and *y*-axis cross on a graph. (p. 70)
origen Punto en donde el eje *x* y el eje *y* se cruzan en una gráfica.

output The result or product from the operation of a technological system. (p. 95)
salida Resultado o producto de la operación de un sistema tecnológico.

patent A legal document issued by a government that gives an inventor exclusive rights to make, use, or sell an invention for a limited time. (p. 105)
patente Documento legal emitido por el gobierno que otorga a un inventor los derechos exclusivos de hacer, usar o vender un invento por un tiempo limitado.

percent error A calculation used to determine how accurate, or close to the true value, an experimental value really is. (p. 65)
error porcentual Cálculo usado para determinar cuán exacto, o cercano al valor verdadero, es realmente un valor.

precision How close a group of measurements are to each other. (p. 62)
precisión Cuán cerca se encuentran un grupo de medidas entre ellas.

predicting The process of forecasting what will happen in the future based on past experience or evidence. (p. 9)
predecir Proceso de pronosticar lo que va a suceder en el futuro, basado en la experiencia pasada o en evidencia.

process A sequence of actions that a technological system undergoes to produce an output. (p. 95)
proceso Secuencia de acciones que experimenta un sistema tecnológico para producir un resultado.

prototype A working model used to test a design. (p. 102)
prototipo Modelo funcional usado para probar un diseño.

qualitative observation An observation that deals with characteristics that cannot be expressed in numbers. (p. 7)
observación cualitativa Observación que se centra en las características que no se pueden expresar con números.

quantitative observation An observation that deals with a number or amount. (p. 7)
observación cuantitativa Observación que se centra en un número o cantidad.

English and Spanish Glossary

R

responding variable The factor that changes as a result of changes to the manipulated, or independent, variable in an experiment; also called dependent variable. (p. 16)
variable de respuesta Factor que cambia como resultado del cambio de la variable manipulada, o independiente, en un experimento; también llamada variable dependiente.

risk-benefit analysis The process of evaluating the possible problems of a technology compared to the expected advantages. (p. 113)
análisis de riesgo y beneficios Proceso por el cual se evalúan los posibles problemas de una tecnología y se compara con las ventajas deseadas.

S

science A way of learning about the natural world through observations and logical reasoning; leads to a body of knowledge. (p. 12)
ciencia Estudio del mundo natural a través de observaciones y del razonamiento lógico; conduce a un conjunto de conocimientos.

scientific inquiry The ongoing process of discovery in science; the diverse ways in which scientists study the natural world and propose explanations based on evidence they gather. (p. 13)
investigación científica Proceso continuo de descubrimiento en la ciencia; diversidad de métodos con los que los científicos estudian el mundo natural y proponen explicaciones del mismo basadas en la evidencia que reúnen.

scientific law A statement that describes what scientists expect to happen every time under a particular set of conditions. (p. 22)
ley científica Enunciado que describe lo que los científicos esperan que suceda cada vez que se da una serie de condiciones determinadas.

scientific literacy The knowledge and understanding of scientific terms and principles required for evaluating information, making personal decisions, and taking part in public affairs. (p. 28)
alfabetismo científico Conocimiento y comprensión de los términos y principios científicos necesarios para evaluar información, tomar decisiones personales y participar en actividades públicas.

scientific theory A well-tested explanation for a wide range of observations or experimental results. (p. 21)
teoría científica Explicación comprobada de una gran variedad de observaciones o resultados de experimentos.

SI (*Système International d'Unités*) International System of Units; a version of the metric system used by scientists all over the world. (p. 45)
SI (*Système International d'Unités*) Sistema Internacional de Unidades; versión del sistema métrico usado por científicos de todo el mundo.

significant figures All the digits in a measurement that have been measured exactly, plus one digit whose value has been estimated. (p. 63)
cifras significativas Todos los dígitos en una medida que se han medido con exactitud, más un dígito cuyo valor se ha estimado.

The length "2.25 m" has three significant figures, while the width "3 m" has one. Therefore, my answer can only have one significant figure.

3 m

skepticism An attitude of doubt. (p. 12)
escepticismo Actitud de duda.

slope The steepness of a graph line; the ratio of the vertical change (the rise) to the horizontal change (the run). (p. 73)
pendiente Inclinación de una gráfica lineal; la razón del cambio vertical (el ascenso) al cambio horizontal (el avance).

system A group of related parts that work together. (p. 95)
sistema Grupo de partes relacionadas que funcionan en conjunto.

technology How people modify the world around them to meet their needs or to solve practical problems. (p. 89)
tecnología Cómo la gente modifica el mundo que la rodea para satisfacer sus necesidades o para solucionar problemas prácticos.

trade-off An exchange in which one benefit is given up in order to obtain another. (p. 101)
intercambio Cambio entre dos o más partes en el cual se renuncia a un beneficio para obtener otro.

troubleshooting The process of analyzing a design problem and finding a way to fix it. (p. 103)
solución de problemas Proceso por el cual se analiza un problema de diseño y se halla una forma de solucionarlo.

variable A factor that can change in an experiment. (p. 16)
variable Factor que puede cambiar en un experimento.

vertical axis (or *y*-axis) A line that runs up and down along the side of a graph, on which the responding variable (or dependent variable) is labeled. (p. 70)
eje vertical (o eje *y*) Recta que va de arriba a abajo en el lado vertical de una gráfica, en la cual se rotula la variable respuesta (o variable dependiente).

volume The amount of space an object takes up. (p. 50)
volumen Cantidad de espacio que ocupa un objeto.

weight A measure of the force of gravity acting on an object. (p. 49)
peso Medida de la fuerza de gravedad que actúa sobre un objeto.

Index

Index

Index

Acknowledgments

Acknowledgment for page 6: Excerpt from *My Life with the Chimpanzees, Revised Edition* by Jane Goodall. Copyright © 1988, 1996 by Byron Preiss Visual Publications, Inc. Text copyright © 1988, 1996 by Jane Goodall. Published by Pocket Books, a division of Simon & Schuster Inc.

Acknowledgment for pages 126–127: From "A Boy's Best Friend" by Isaac Asimov. Reprinted from *Boys' Life,* March 1975.

Staff Credits

Scott Andrews, Jennifer Angel, Laura Baselice, Carolyn Belanger, Barbara A. Bertell, Suzanne Biron, Peggy Bliss, Stephanie Bradley, James Brady, Anne M. Bray, Kerry Cashman, Jonathan Cheney, Joshua D. Clapper, Lisa J. Clark, Bob Craton, Patricia Cully, Patricia M. Dambry, Kathy Dempsey, Emily Ellen, Thomas Ferreira, Jonathan Fisher, Patricia Fromkin, Paul Gagnon, Robert Graham, Ellen Granter, Barbara Hollingdale, Etta Jacobs, Linda Johnson, Anne Jones, John Judge, Kevin Keane, Kelly Kelliher, Toby Klang, Russ Lappa, Carolyn Lock, Rebecca Loveys, Constance J. McCarty, Carolyn B. McGuire, Ranida Touranont McKneally, Anne McLaughlin, Eve Melnechuk, Tania Mlawer, Janet Morris, Francine Neumann, Marie Opera, Jill Ort, Joan Paley, Dorothy Preston, Rashid Ross, Siri Schwartzman, Laurel Smith, Emily Soltanoff, Jennifer A. Teece, Diane Walsh, Amanda M. Watters, Merce Wilczek, Amy Winchester, Char Lyn Yeakley. **Additional Credits** Tara Allamilla, Terence Hegarty, Louise Gachet, Andrea Golden, Stephanie Rogers, Kim Schmidt, Joan Tobin.

Illustration

Kerry Cashman: 10–11t, 18, 20, 55, 66, 67, 81, 84, 90, 91, 94, 108–109; **John Ceballos:** 91–93; **John Edwards:** 68, 69, 70–71; **Gary Glover:** 58–59, 98, 99, 100–101, 102–103, 104–105; **Barbara Hollingdale:** 13; **Richard McMahon:** 46–47, 54, 112–113, 120; **Kim and James Neale:** 61, 63, 64; **XNR Productions:** 11b. **All charts and graphs by Matt Mayerchak.**

Photography

Photo Research Paula Wehde
Cover image top, Rosenfeld Images Ltd./Science Photo Library; **bottom,** Gary S. and Vivian Chapman/Getty Images.

Page vi, SPL/Photo Researchers, Inc.; **vii,** Richard Haynes; **viii tl,** Getty Images, Inc.; **viii tr,** Dorling Kindersley; **viii b,** Richard Haynes; **x–1,** Alan S. Weiner; **1 both,** Johnson Research and Development Co.; **2t,** Lonnie G. Johnson; **2b,** Robin Samper; **3l,** Johnson Research and Development Co.; **3m,** Lonnie G. Johnson; **3r,** Lonnie G. Johnson.

Chapter 1
Pages 4–5, Barrett and MacKay; **5 inset,** Richard Haynes; **7t,** Michael Nichols/National Geographic Society; **7b,** Manoh Shah/Getty Images, Inc.; **8,** K. & K. Ammann/Bruce Coleman, Inc.; **9,** Wild Chimpanzees.org; **10t,** Wild Chimpanzees.org; **10b,** Dorling Kindersley; **11l,** Irven De Vore/Anthrophoto File; **11r,** Adrian Warren/Lastrefuge.co.uk; **12,** Gay Bumgarner/Visuals Unlimited; **13t,** Richard Haynes; **13b,** M.T. Frazier/Photo Researchers, Inc.; **14,** Richard Haynes; **15,** Richard Haynes; **16–17,** Richard Haynes; **18,** Richard Haynes; **19,** Richard Haynes; **20 all,** Richard Haynes; **21,** Detlev Van Ravensway/SPL/Photo Researchers, Inc.; **22,** Shirley Church/Photo Researchers, Inc.; **23 both,** Richard Haynes; **24,** David Young-Wolff/PhotoEdit; **25,** Bob Daemmrich; **26,** Dana White/PhotoEdit; **27,** Superstock, Inc.; **28–29,** Panoramic Images; **29t inset,** Linda Burton/Robertstock; **29b inset,** Superstock/PictureQuest; **30,** Photri, Inc.; **31l,** SPL/Photo Researchers, Inc.; **31r,** Wolfgang Kaehler/Corbis; **32,** SPL/Photo Researchers, Inc.; **33 all,** NASA; **34t,** ARS; **34bl,** ARS; **34bm,** ARS; **34br,** USDA; **35,** Russ Lappa; **36l,** Jeff Zaruba/Corbis; **36r,** Bob Daemmrich Photography, Inc.; **37l,** Bill Cornett; **37r,** PictureQuest; **38t,** Manoh Shah/ Getty Images, Inc.; **38b,** Richard Haynes; **40,** Renee Stockdale/Animals Animals/Earth Scenes.

Chapter 2
Pages 42–43, Flip Nicklin/Minden Pictures; **43 inset,** Richard Haynes; **44b,** David Young-Wolf/PhotoEdit; **44t,** Richard Haynes; **45,** Richard Haynes; **46l,** Bettmann/Corbis; **46m,** Dorling Kindersley; **46r,** The Art Archive/The Picture Desk, Inc.; **47l,** Bridgeman Art Library; **47m,** Science & Society Picture Library; **47r,** Bureau of International Weights & Measures; **48,** Richard Haynes; **49,** Richard Haynes; **50 both,** Richard Haynes; **51,** Richard Haynes; **52,** Richard Haynes; **53 both,** Richard Haynes; **54,** Richard Haynes; **56,** Richard Haynes; **57,** Richard Haynes; **60,** Richard Haynes; **61,** Kevin Fleming/Corbis; **62 all,** Richard Haynes; **66–67,** Eric Haucke/Greg Ochocki Productions/Photo Researchers, Inc.; **69,** Richard Haynes; **72l,** Richard Haynes; **72r,** Getty Images, Inc.; **73 both,** Stephen Oliver/Dorling Kindersley; **74l,** Mark C. Burnett/Photo Researchers, Inc.; **74r,** Dr. K.S. Kim/Peter Arnold, Inc.; **75l,** Royalty-Free/Corbis; **75m,** Index Stock Imagery, Inc.; **75r,** Dorling Kindersley; **76,** Richard Haynes; **77b,** David Young-Wolf/PhotoEdit; **77t,** Index Stock Imagery, Inc.; **78,** Richard Haynes; **79,** Richard Haynes; **80,** Myrleen Ferguson Cate/PhotoEdit; **82t,** Royalty-Free/Corbis; **82b,** Index Stock Imagery, Inc.

Chapter 3
Pages 86–87, Hank Morgan/Photo Researchers, Inc; **87 inset,** Richard Haynes; **88b,** Corbis; **88tl,** Getty Images, Inc.; **88tm,** Casio, Inc.; **88tml,** Corbis; **88tmr,** Corbis; **88tr,** Dorling Kindersley; **89l,** Advertising Archive/The Picture Desk, Inc.; **89m,** Advertising Archive; **89r,** The Granger Collection; **90l,** Masterfile; **90r,** Richard Haynes; **91l,** Peter A. Simon/Corbis; **91m,** Phototake; **91r,** Photo Researchers; **94l,** David Young-Wolf/PhotoEdit; **94r,** Richard Haynes; **96 both,** Richard Haynes; **97 both,** Richard Haynes; **99,** Dorling Kindersley; **100,** Dorling Kindersley; **101,** Dorling Kindersley; **102,** NASA/Photo Researchers, Inc.; **104t,** Dorling Kindersley; **104b,** Fisher/Thatcher/Getty Images, Inc.; **106,** Richard Haynes; **107,** Richard Haynes; **108l inset,** Bridgeman Art Library; **108r inset,** Hulton Archive/Getty Images Inc.; **108–109b,** Richard Haynes; **109 inset,** PictureQuest; **110l,** SupersStock, Inc.; **110r,** Richard Haynes; **112l,** The Art Archive; **112m,** Getty Images, Inc.; **112r,** BATA Shoe Museum; **113l,** Corbis; **113ml,** Index Stock Imagery, Inc.; **113mr,** Fisher/Thatcher/Getty Images, Inc.; **113r,** SPL/Photo Researchers; **114,** Corbis; **116,** Richard Haynes; **118l,** Richard Haynes; **118,** Dorling Kindersley.

Page 122 both, Peter Menzel/Stock Boston; **123,** NASA; **124t,** NASA/Carnegie Mellon University/SPL/Photo Researchers, Inc.; **124m,** Australian Centre for Field Robotics; **124b,** Kim Kyung-Hoon/Corbis; **125,** AP/Wide World Photos; **126l,** Rick Friedman/Black Star; **126–127,** Attila Hejja/Corbis; **128,** Tony Freeman/PhotoEdit; **129t,** Russ Lappa; **129m,** Richard Haynes; **129b,** Russ Lappa; **130,** Richard Haynes; **132,** Richard Haynes; **134,** Morton Beebe/Corbis; **135,** Catherine Karnow/Corbis; **137t,** Dorling Kindersley Media Library; **137b,** Richard Haynes; **139,** Image Stop/Phototake; **142,** Richard Haynes; **149,** Richard Haynes; **150,** Russ Lappa; **151 both,** Russ Lappa; **152,** Richard Haynes; **153,** Richard Haynes; **154b,** K. & K. Ammann/Bruce Coleman, Inc.; **154t,** Mark C. Burnett/Photo Researchers, Inc.; **156,** Superstock; **157,** SPL/Photo Researchers, Inc.